What People are Saying...

"David Dawson's *The Priesthood of Every Believer* is the finest treatise I have seen on this subject. His lifetime ministry as a global teacher and trainer of those who are 'equipping the saints' uniquely qualifies him to write this outstanding explanation of one of the key issues of our day. As I travel around the world addressing Christian business leaders, I find this to be a critical matter for examination."

Kent Humphreys
Christ@Work
Oklahoma City, Oklahoma

"I have worked with Dave Dawson for over thirty years as an editor and graphic designer of the ***Equipping The Saints*** training curriculum. I have also traveled extensively with him training leaders in many countries, in addition to my own ministry among business and professional leaders in the marketplace. This present work, ***The Priesthood of Every Believer***, is a vital matter that has been nearly abandoned by scholars, and is crucially needed in the training of Christian leaders today. I heartily commend this study for your consideration."

Gordon E. Adams
Vision Foundation Inc.
Knoxville, Tennessee

We have needed Dave's teaching on "The Priesthood of Every Believer" and the scriptural mapping to stir the soul of evangelical ignorance. This study is literally a breath of fresh air for today's churches and Spirit-led believers. In my travel to many nations and working with thousands of churches I have found Christian leaders who simply do not understand and have not been taught this critical study from God's Word. And we wonder why there is no evidence of divine power in the lives of those who are coming to Christ or have been believers for years!

Roger D. McCasland, President
International Teaching Ministry,
Great Commission Ministries

By David L. Dawson

the PRIesтHOOD of every BeLIeveR

Resolving the Clergy/Laity Distinction

Acknowledgments

To God, who guides me to certain topics and compels me to write on these subjects.

To my wife, Mary, who encourages me in every project God puts on my heart.

To a team of very gifted colaborers who make it possible for a less gifted one to produce a book—especially to Kent Humphreys who believed in this concept and made it possible for me to print the first edition.

I am also grateful to:
- Molly Ragan, who computerized my written notes.
- Gordon Adams and my son, D. R. Dawson, who carefully edited my thoughts for clarity and easier reading.
- A team of people who have read and made excellent suggestions which have strengthened the thesis of this book:
  Rev. Dwain Camp
  Rev. Kenneth Durst
  Rev. Dave Semmelbeck
  Rev. Doyle Sumrall
  Rev. Walt Millet
  Rev. Walter Hendricksen
  Dr. Randy Weyeneth, PhD
  Ben Bennett
  Dan Walters

- My colaborers, whose prayers and gifts make it possible for me to represent their ministry to you.
- Sheri Seawright, whose layout makes this book readable.
- Chad Rogez, who designed the cover for this book.

Table
of Contents

Foreword

When I became a Christian in 1956, I began to hear a few friends speak about a concept they referred to as the priesthood of every believer. It was a completely new idea to me; I could not recall it being taught in any church I ever attended. In fact, the model I observed and was taught was a model in which the pastor and church leaders were considered priests while the rest of us were mere laymen. I later came to realize most churches practice what is referred to as a *clergy/laity model of ministry*.

Early in my Christian life I met and began discipleship training with The Navigators. Although they didn't specifically speak about the priesthood of every believer, they did practice it. Through their ministry, God gave me a vision for the world and helped me to understand that I had a personal and important role in the fulfilling of the Great Commission. I learned how to develop my own relationship with God and how to win and disciple others.

In 1983—over 25 years after my own conversion—my personal study of the Scripture led me to again explore the concept. I wrote a paper on the subject and taught it for three years in my *Equipping The Saints (ETS)* Pastor Training Seminars. With each succeeding presentation, I attempted to hone this subject in an effort to bring light rather than heat to the subject. At that time I decided to make it a part of the ETS Vision in Lesson Three of the course. I never intended to address this doctrine further.

In July 2007, a pastor friend of mine gave me a book that dealt with the matter of the priesthood of the believer. The author led me to a Bible passage that became the starting point of a five-month re-examination of the doctrine. It became increasingly clear to me that this teaching is inextricably connected to our personal identity as believers. God has created us to be His *kings* and *priests* (Revelation 1:5,6). This simple truth answers three essential questions:

- *Who* am I?
- *Why* are we here?
- *What* is God's will for our lives?

A Christian's true identity is displaced when he is taught that church leaders (clergy) are the only real priests. This theology purports that *the clergy are the activists in ministry and that laypeople are only there to offer support from the sidelines.* The result is a loss of identity, and a loss of direction and purpose in life. Every believer needs to be able to articulate *who* he is, *why* he is here, and *what* he is supposed to be doing while on earth.

The Spirit of God has compelled me to take up my pen and begin to write again about the priesthood of every believer in an attempt to help resolve the distinction between clergy and laity. My prayer is that this book will be used by God to restore the reader to his or her God-given identity as a Priest of God and that every believer would be empowered for ministry.

David L. Dawson
Dallas, Texas 2008

Introduction

How did the church evolve from the original priesthood of every believer to the current clergy/laity structure? To find the answer to this crucial question, we need to follow very carefully the historical progression of the priesthood revealed for us in Scripture, beginning in the Old Testament, and concluding in the New Testament.

Definition of a Priest

The Old Testament Hebrew word for priest means 'one who stands,' particularly referring to standing before an altar. A biblical priest had two primary responsibilities:

1) To represent God to mankind

2) To intercede for mankind before God

Priests often received instructions (called oracles) from God and then relayed that information to the people as intermediaries.

In Chapter 1, we will trace the development of the priesthood in the Old Testament, beginning in the Garden of Eden, continuing through to Moses at Mt. Sinai and to the end of the Old Testament with the book of Malachi.

In Chapter 2, we will investigate the priesthood as it evolved in the New Testament with the life and death of Jesus Christ, and its transmission through the early disciples of Christ.

1

Priesthood in the Old Testament

Garden of Eden to Mt. Sinai
Before Sin: Genesis 1:1 – Genesis 3:13

Before sin entered the world, Adam and Eve lived in a beautiful and harmonious relationship with God. Technically, there was no need for a priest. However, Adam *functioned* as a priest because he had received instructions from God and bore responsibility to pass those instructions on to Eve and others who came after her. Adam was obedient and taught Eve about the *Tree of Knowledge of Good and Evil*. This is evident, for when she was confronted by Satan, she made this statement, "If we eat from this tree we will surely die."

Sin and the Tree of Knowledge
Genesis 3:14 – Exodus 18

Once Adam and Eve had been warned about the Tree of Knowledge, but chose to eat nonetheless, sin entered the world. Mankind became spiritually dead and cut off from fellowship and communion with the Father. However, in God's love and grace toward us, mankind indirectly benefited from Satan's curse by God's promise.

> *And I will put enmity between you and the woman, and between your seed and her Seed; He shall bruise your head, and you shall bruise His heel.*
> *Genesis 3:15*

Satan was told that from the seed, or offspring, of a woman, God was going to give a Seed. This Seed would be a *Messiah*, or *Savior*, who would die as a substitute in our place. His death would pay sin's debt and restore us into right relationship with God. God was willing to accept the blood of an animal until the future sacrifice of Christ would be made. Adam and Eve had tried to cover their nakedness with the leaves from the Garden. Before God expelled them, He covered them with the skin of an animal. This was the first blood sacrifice for sin. Centuries later, the author of Hebrews reminds us:

> *And according to the law almost all things are purged with blood, and without shedding of blood there is no remission.*
> *Hebrews 9:22*

Mankind was expelled from the Garden of Eden because there was a Tree of Life. If Adam and Eve had eaten of this tree in their

sinful condition, they would have lived forever with no hope of being restored to a personal relationship with God. It would be another 2,500 years before God would carefully explain His plan of restoration to the nation of Israel.

Mankind Functioning as Their Own Priests

Cain and Abel: Genesis 4

Adam and Eve's sons began to build altars and offer sacrifices. Cain was a farmer and offered the fruit of the ground, but the ground had been cursed by God (Gen. 3:17). It was not a blood sacrifice and was rejected. By contrast, Abel, who was a shepherd, offered a blood sacrifice, and God accepted it. Scripture does not tell us how Abel knew to offer a blood sacrifice. He may have learned it from God's example, or from observing Adam carrying out his priestly responsibilities. Further, Adam may have instructed him how to offer sacrifices.

Noah: Genesis 8

In Genesis 8, the very first thing Noah did when disembarking from the Ark was to build an altar and offer a blood sacrifice to God. Noah was given the same instructions that God had originally given to Adam.

Abram to Abraham: Genesis 12-24

Some Jewish Rabbis tell us that by the time Abram appeared on the stage of ancient history, over 2,000 years had passed. Though mankind had rebelled against God, His love for them had never wavered. God's plan was to find someone He could use to carry this message of love. God found in Abram a man with whom He could build a relationship. When God spoke, Abram listened, believed and demonstrated willingness for God to use him. So, God chose Abram, changed his name to Abraham, and made him a promise: He would make of him a great nation, which would become a blessing to the entire world. God wanted to teach Israel about Himself, as well as about His love for all creation. This nation would then be made a *nation of priests* who would carry the message of His love to all the nations of the world. Israel would provide the context for the Messiah to be born into the world to pay sin's debt, in order for mankind to be restored once again into right relationship with God.

Now the Lord had said to Abram: "Get out of your country, from your kindred and from your father's house, to a land that I will show you. I will make you a great nation; I will bless you and make your name great; and you shall be a blessing. I will bless those who bless you, and I will curse him who curses you; and in you all the families of the earth shall be blessed."
Genesis 12:1-3

Throughout his lifetime, Abraham built altars and offered sacrifices directly to God. God had a special plan for this nation He was going to raise up through Abraham. However, it would be another 500 years before God would reveal this plan to anyone. A part of God's plan included a 430-year sojourn in Egypt.

*From the time of the Garden of Eden until Mt. Sinai **any man in any place could build an altar and offer his sacrifice directly to God. Every man functioned as a priest in his own right.***

Deliverance of Abraham's Nation

When God delivered Israel from their 400-year bondage, they were in no condition to consummate the plan God had conceived for them. Moses, their new leader, took them to Mt. Sinai so that God could reveal His plan and prepare them for the ministry. After 400 years of bondage, they were no more than a nation of slaves with little confidence in the promises that were given them through Abraham. God therefore began to prepare Israel through some of the greatest demonstrations of power the world had ever witnessed.

The people of God saw Him display His love for them as the seas opened and closed on their enemies. When they needed water for their journey, they experienced God's provision of water from a rock. He began to supply quail and manna when their food had run out and defeated an army that had come against them as they journeyed toward Mt. Sinai. They witnessed God Himself leading them by a cloud during the day and a pillar of fire by night. It might be said that the confidence that had disappeared during the 400 years of bondage was gradually restored by the time they reached the Holy Mountain.

In the years to come they would see God use them as an instrument of judgment on the Canaanites, who had rejected Him. This nation had polluted themselves with every conceivable demonic practice. Now God intended to use Israel as a lighthouse to guide other polluted nations back to Himself. He still loved those evil nations, and wanted to use Israel to demonstrate His love. God was very clear when He gave this promise to Abraham: *"You will become a blessing to all the nations of the world."* Just as God loved us while we were yet sinners, so God loved the nations of the world.

p^{the}RíestHOOD
^{of}eveRy BeLieveR

The Plan for the Nations

After such an awesome display of power and love, there must have been a growing curiosity among the Hebrew nation as to what God had in mind for them. God revealed His plan to Moses, and directed him to guide the people into a covenant agreement with this plan. It was a covenant contingent upon Israel's obedience.

And Moses went up to God, and the Lord called to him from the mountain saying, "Thus you shall say to the house of Jacob, and tell the children of Israel: You have seen what I did to the Egyptians, and how I bore you on eagles' wings and brought you to Myself. Now therefore, if you will indeed obey My voice and keep My covenant, then you shall be a special treasure to Me above all people; for all the earth is Mine. ***And you shall be to Me a kingdom of priests*** *and a holy nation. These are the words which you shall speak to the children of Israel." So Moses came and called for the elders of the people, and laid before them all these words which the Lord commanded him. Then all the people answered together and said, "All that the Lord has spoken we will do." So Moses brought back the words of the people to the Lord.*

Exodus 19:3-8

From this passage, it is eminently clear that Israel was to become a ***kingdom of priests***. As they were taught and led by God they were to function in a mediatory role as a lighthouse or guide to carry the message of God's love to the Gentile nations about them. The Father's plan was that they were to be the messengers by which He would bring the knowledge of salvation to the world, since that is the major role of a priest.

Some believe God's intention for Israel's priesthood is not expounded upon in greater detail in the Old Testament primarily *because they failed to live in obedience to what they promised and committed themselves to do* (Exodus 19). Since they did not live in accordance with the light they were given, God did not grant them more. The Old Testament records Israel's misguided efforts to achieve what they *thought* God wanted. Their modification of God's original plan resulted in disaster, and the historical ramifications of their disobedience have echoed through the corridors of time to this day.

My conclusions regarding Israel's failure to fully comply with God's plan are based on a contrast between the *kingdom of priests* mentioned here and the teachings of Jesus Christ concerning the priesthood in the New Testament. Both priesthoods carried the same mediatory responsibility of instructing others about God's love for them and His plan for their salvation. The Bible, from beginning to end is the story of God's restoration of fallen mankind to a relationship with Himself through Jesus' death upon the cross. An important component of God's plan is the means by which He intends this message to be propagated.

As a result of the covenant described in Exodus 19, Israel was transformed from a nation of *slaves* into a nation of *priests*. We have seen that men had always functioned in a priestly capacity, but this is the first time God had spoken directly to the issue. On four occasions—from the Garden of Eden to Mt. Sinai—the word priest appears:

- Genesis 14:18 speaks of Melchizedek as the priest of the most High God.

- Genesis 41:45 records the fact that Joseph was married to the daughter of Potipherah, the priest of On.

- In Genesis 47:22, we are told that Joseph did not purchase the priests' land for Pharaoh.

- Exodus 18:1 describes Jethro as the priest of Midian.

There is no explanation in any of these passages of what a priest *is* or *does*, and no word about *who* can be a priest or *who is to be* a priest. At Mt. Sinai God spoke very clearly regarding the matter of the priesthood, and gave specific, detailed instructions that shed light on these questions.

Some refer to Israel's call to become a kingdom of priests as the Law of First Intent. God, for the first time in Scripture, declared His intention for Israel to become a *nation of priests*. From this time forward we must understand Israel's priesthood as a *national responsibility*. When God made Israel vocationally a nation of priests, He probably didn't envision everyone wearing a collar or robe, or holding an ecclesiastical office. But He must have intended that each was to be a guide, someone fully capable of representing His love to other people.

The thesis of this book is that the Law of First Intent and God's intention for Israel to be a kingdom of priests is fully illuminated by the New Testament and the priestly role each disciple of Jesus is expected to play.

Instructions for Israel's Priesthood

God's directives governing the priesthood were given to Israel in several ways. First, the nation received the Ten Commandments.

Of the Ten, the first four were meant to guard their relationship with God. The next six were intended to guard their relationships with other people and nations. Violation of the commandments voided ministry to others. God also gave Israel a very detailed set of instructions in the form of a Triune Code (Moral, Spiritual and Social). This code elevated them into the most advanced nation of the world. These mandates are detailed in the books of Exodus, Leviticus, Numbers and Deuteronomy. This code was predicated upon the **Shema**, the central tenet of Judaism. The **Shema** was given to help people focus on God and the love He offered them. It was to draw them into intimacy and fellowship.

"Hear, O Israel: The LORD our God, the LORD is one! You shall love the LORD your God with all your heart, with all your soul, and with all your strength. And these words which I command you today shall be in your heart. You shall teach them diligently to your children, and shall talk of them when you sit in your house, when you walk by the way, when you lie down, and when you rise up."

Deuteronomy 6:4-7

The **Shema** says that the Law or Commandments were to be **written upon the hearts of the people**—not just on the scrolls of the Torah. The people of Israel were to teach God's Word diligently to their children by talking about it when they were sitting in their homes, or out walking—at night before retiring and upon rising in the morning. The **Shema** was to be a gentle reminder of God's love, drawing them ever more closely into intimate fellowship with Him. Another portion of the Law prescribed observances (feasts, sacrifices, Holy Days) that were to be followed at least until the Messiah completed His work of redemption. Unfortunately, these observances tended to become the primary focus, creating a religion to follow rather than a relationship to be enjoyed. The **Shema** remains a perfect expression of the intended balance between God's love for the people and their obedience to Him.

Special Functions of the Levitical Priests

God gave Aaron and his sons special responsibilities within the tribe of Levi. The Levites cared for the spiritual needs of the other eleven tribes, and, together they were to devote themselves to reaching the nations. Although the Levites led Israel in worship, intercession, etc., the other eleven tribes remained responsible to represent God to the nations, making Israel the lighthouse that God intended. Since they were the key to reaching the world with the message of salvation, Israel enjoyed special favor with God. The gifted leaders of the Old Testament seem to have operated in much the same way that the apostles, prophets, evangelists, pastors and teachers of the New Testament operated centuries later. That is, they were responsible to equip the saints (the tribes) in the work of ministry so that they could carry out their priestly functions.

Here are some examples of responsibilities only Levitical priests could perform on behalf of Israel:

Moses: Moses was a *Prophet*, but functioned as God's *priest* to Israel.

Aaron: Aaron was the High Priest. On the Day of Atonement only he could enter the Holy of Holies and offer a blood sacrifice for the sins of the nation.

Aaron's Sons: They alone could minister at the altar and offer the sacrifice for the people. Mankind could no longer build their own altars and offer their own sacrifices.

Levitical Priests: They were the caretakers of the Tabernacle and responsible for all aspects of its upkeep.

The Levites were never intended to usurp the rights and responsibilities of the other tribes, or to carry out their priestly functions for them. Their duties emphasized what they were to do and not who they were positionally. In reality, these duties made the Levitical priests servants to the other eleven tribes.

Nowhere in the Old Testament are we ever taught that the Levitical priests' functions made them a distinct, separate or special priesthood. Levitical is an *adjective* and does not change the meaning of the *noun* priest. The word Levitical describes the ***functions*** these priests were to carry out.

The Old Testament Levitical priesthood was instituted as a forerunner of Christ to come. His Melchizedekian Priesthood supersedes it in every way. The book of Hebrews teaches that this new priesthood is based upon better promises, a better covenant, a better sacrifice and, without question, a better priest. The Levitical priesthood, in the heart and mind of God, was always a ***temporary arrangement***—a foreshadowing of a future priesthood to be established by Jesus, the Messiah. This New Covenant was prophesied by the Prophet Jeremiah (Jeremiah 31:31). The book of Hebrews tells us that the New Covenant was fulfilled in Christ and rendered the Levitical Priesthood obsolete. Under the New Covenant, the death of the promised Messiah established a New Priesthood in which **all believers** are priests under Jesus Christ, our High Priest.

> *When He said, "A new covenant," He has made the first obsolete. But whatever is becoming obsolete and growing old is ready to disappear.*
> *Hebrews 8:13 (NASB)*

As we saw in Exodus 19, the Israelites were to be a nation of priests. However the Levitical priesthood was intended to function within God's larger plan for the nation of Israel, its role is annulled by the New Testament.

Israel's Acceptance

We note that in Exodus 19 the nation of Israel was quick to respond to God's offer to become a nation of priests: *"All that the Lord hath spoken we will do."* But Israel often seemed reluctant to reach out to the nations with the offer of God's blessing. As we study the Old Testament, we see little contact between Israel and the neighboring nations other than for meeting Israel's material needs. Spiritually, the eleven tribes appear happy to allow the Levitical tribe, with its special functions, to assume all priestly responsibility.

God's Plan Modified

It appears the Levitical priests were willing to assume the rights and responsibilities intended for the other tribes. Soon a form of clergy/laity relationship began to emerge and dominate the Old Testament model of ministry. We surmise that this was never God's will and plan. Israel's disobedience and readiness to abandon God's plan was contrary to what they had promised. In effect, they modified God's plan, restructuring the **Kingdom** of priests into a **Tribe** of priests.

This was a sure recipe for disaster. Their one-year sojourn at Mt. Sinai illustrates this perfectly.

Mt. Sinai to Malachi: Historical Overview

At Mt. Sinai, in Moses' absence, Aaron, the High Priest, made a golden calf, and he and his sons led the nation into the worship of this idol. This propelled God's nation of priests down a path of disobedience, idolatry and apostasy. Within one year, their rebellion turned an eleven-day journey into the Promised Land into forty years of wandering in the desert. It also resulted in the death of every disobedient priest over 20 years of age. However, under the leadership of Joshua, the successor to Moses, the nation improved dramatically.

God had given mankind a free will, and He allowed them to use it, which accounts for the many poor choices His people made during the years of history recorded in Samuel, Kings and Chronicles. It is also obvious from these accounts that God was gracious and merciful, sending prophets and judges to call them to account when they wandered from His plan. Again and again, He nudged and prodded His people lovingly, as He longed for them to fulfill their appointed destiny. He eventually sent them into exile, and the tribes were divided, further sealing their fate and destroying the ideal of a priestly kingdom that was never fully realized by the nation of Israel.

Thankfully, God's plan for the redemption of the world was not thwarted by the failure of Israel to fulfill its part of the conditional covenant it had agreed to at Mt. Sinai.

The period from the Garden of Eden to Mt. Sinai could be characterized as follows: *Any man in any place could build his altar and offer his sacrifice directly to God*. We might characterize the period of Israel's history from Mt. Sinai to Malachi as a time when *only special people in special places could build altars and offer sacrifices on behalf of the people of God*.

2

Priesthood in the New Testament

Jesus Christ came to earth 1,500 years after God revealed His plan for His people at Mt. Sinai. The Levitical tribe continued to pursue a self-serving agenda. The very priests who should have eagerly received the long-awaited Messiah chose rather to reject Him. Jesus, in spite of the signs, wonders, and miracles—which authenticated Him as the Messiah—could not penetrate their hearts of stone. The Levites told the people, This is not the Messiah. The powers which He has displayed are not divine, but demonic. It was these very priests who engineered the crucifixion of the Son of God through the agency of the Roman government. As a result, they were no longer fit to represent God, neither to the eleven tribes nor to the other nations of the world. These facts are documented in the four Gospels.

pR$\overset{the}{\text{i}}$estHOOD
^{of}eveRy BeLieveR

When Jesus came to earth His primary ministry was two-fold:

- The work of redemption,
- The training of the Twelve

The Work of Redemption

Jesus Christ came as the promised Messiah. He was the Seed of the woman who would crush Satan's head (Genesis 3:15)—or undo what Satan had done to destroy mankind's relationship with God. Jesus came to die as a substitute in mankind's place to pay the penalty for sin. The writer of Hebrews tells us that Jesus was our High Priest:

> But Christ came as High Priest of the good things to come, with the greater and more perfect tabernacle not made with hands, that is, not of this creation. Not with the blood of goats and calves, but with His own blood He entered the Most Holy Place once for all, having obtained eternal redemption. For if the blood of bulls and goats and the ashes of a heifer, sprinkling the unclean, sanctifies for the purifying of the flesh, how much more shall the blood of Christ, who through the eternal Spirit offered Himself without spot to God, purge your conscience from dead works to serve the living God?
>
> *Hebrews 9:11-14*

On Passover, Jesus symbolically entered the Holy of Holies and sprinkled His own blood upon the mercy seat for the sins of the nations. At that moment His blood paid the debt of sin so that believers in Christ could be restored to the relationship with God that mankind enjoyed before sin entered the world. Jesus, as the Perfect Man, was allowed to die for the sins of humanity. Yet, in

His divinity, He was allowed to die for the sins of **all** mankind. Paul's letter to the Romans states it clearly and simply:

Therefore, as through one man's offense judgment came to all men, resulting in condemnation, even so through one Man's righteous act the free gift came to all men, resulting in justification of life. For as by one man's disobedience many were made sinners, so also by one Man's obedience many will be made righteous.
Romans 5:18-19

Jesus had spent His entire earthly life demonstrating to the world that He was the perfect spotless lamb without blemish. In six short but brutal hours on the cross, He purchased with His blood our eternal redemption and justification before God the Father.

The Training of the Twelve

When Jesus began His earthly ministry, He was aware that God had prepared work for Him to do before His final work of redemption. In the Garden of Gethsemane Jesus prayed:

I have glorified You on the earth. I have finished the work which You have given Me to do.
John 17:4

Some have speculated that the obedient life and ministry of Jesus Christ automatically reversed a 1500-year error that began at Mt. Sinai. Israel had turned God's intended **nation** of priests into a **tribe** of priests. In so doing, they created something that would gradually evolve into the **clergy/laity** model that exists today. God was not willing for this error to be carried into the

New Testament church. When Christ said, "Upon this rock I will build my church," He never intended a clergy/laity configuration. Jesus Himself was to be the Rock, and the church that He came to establish was to be built on the Law of First Intent—the priesthood of every believer. It was to be a ***kingdom of priests***.

During His life, Jesus was to raise up a band of disciples, train them to be priests, and then help them train and raise up the next generation of priests. God yearned for priests who understood His will and the Law of First Intent. Since Jesus didn't write out His plan for training the disciples to become priests, we depend on those disciples whom He trained to help us understand what was involved in their priestly training.

Vision

Perhaps Jesus' greatest strength in His humanity was a clear vision of His calling and purpose:

- Jesus knew ***Who*** He was—He was the Messiah.
- Jesus knew ***Why*** He was here—the work of redemption, and the training of the Twelve.
- Jesus knew ***What*** he had to do—make disciples who could make and train a kingdom of priests who understood God's will and objective for their earthly lives.

Jesus realized that He faced a people that had lost their original vision—they had forfeited their identity. In the Law of First Intent, they had been given the same vision as Jesus had:

- ***Who*** they were—priests.
- ***Why*** they were here—to carry out their priestly functions.

- **What** they were supposed to be doing—acting as guides and lighthouses as they represented God's love to the entire world.

When Israel distorted God's plan and will for their lives, they abdicated their primary role in God's great plan of redemption. They rejected the very things that would have brought meaning, purpose and joy to their lives. Their compromise left them adrift, like a ship on the stormy sea of life without map or rudder. When the masses met Jesus, they saw Him as a **Lighthouse** in the storm. He taught with such power and authority because He knew **Who** He was, **Why** He was here, and **What** He had to do to restore their relationship with God. As they began to follow Him, Christ clarified the nature of the priesthood He was calling them to. Peter reminds us of that priesthood, using language that recalls the covenant God made with his people in Exodus 19:3-8.

*You also, as living stones, are being built up into a spiritual house, **a holy priesthood**, to offer up spiritual sacrifices acceptable to God through Jesus Christ.*
I Peter 2:5

*But you are a chosen generation, **a royal priesthood**, a holy nation, His own special people, that you may proclaim the praises of Him who called you out of darkness into His marvelous light.*
I Peter 2:9

The Apostle John, who penned the affirmation of the Deity of Jesus in John 1:1-3, makes an equally strident affirmation in Revelation of who we are.

John, to the seven churches which are in Asia: Grace to you and peace from Him Who is and who was and who *is to come, and from the seven Spirits who are before His throne, and from Jesus Christ, the faithful witness, the firstborn from the dead, and the ruler over the kings of the earth. To Him who loved us and washed us from our sins in His own blood, and has made us **kings** and **priests** to His God and Father, to Him be glory and dominion forever and ever. Amen.*

Revelation 1:4-6

The Lord Jesus further clarifies our understanding of the New Testament priesthood of every believer when He states in John's Gospel that we are *"chosen and ordained"* for the work of ministry (it is interesting the term ordination is applied to *all believers*!).

*Ye have not chosen me, but I have **chosen** you, and **ordained** you, that ye should go and bring forth fruit, and that your fruit should remain: that whatsoever ye shall ask of the Father in my name, He may give it you.*

John 15:16 (KJV)

Jesus gave final marching orders to His band of disciples: They were to *make disciples of all the nations of the world.* These disciples knew *Who* they were—priests, who were called to multiply themselves by establishing a *kingdom of priests*. The disciples made Jesus' vision their own vision and taught succeeding generations to do the same. The building of God's kingdom was to take priority over their own interests.

But seek first the kingdom of God and His righteousness, and all these things shall be added to you.

Matthew 6:33

The Essence of Jesus' Priestly Training

Three days before His crucifixion, in a confrontation with the Sadducees and Pharisees, Jesus distills the essence of His training in Matthew's Gospel:

> *Jesus said to him, "You shall love the Lord your God with all your heart, with all your soul, and with all your mind. This is the first and great commandment. And the second is like it: You shall love your neighbor as yourself. On these two commandments hang all the Law and the Prophets."*
>
> *Matthew 22:37-40*

- Jesus taught men to love God with the totality of their lives. He called this the first and Greatest Commandment. This is the **Shema.** It focuses on our *personal relationship with God.*

- Jesus taught men to *love their neighbors as they love themselves.* This is usually referred to as the Great Commission. It focuses on developing relationships with others with a view to carrying out **our priestly function**—to represent God's love to other people through evangelism and disciplemaking.

Jesus taught that all God intends for our priesthood and ministry to others was summarized in these two commandments. We can conclude that:

- The training is not difficult.

- Every person is capable of fulfilling these two commandments.

Following is a simple illustration called the Wheel that will help us understand and teach others about the work of ministry.

The Word

Evangelism   GREAT JESUS COMMISSION   Discipleship

Prayer

This illustration is included primarily for those who have questions about how to disciple others. We will briefly describe some of the principles involved in the discipleship process. The Wheel captures what Jesus was trying to communicate in Matthew 22. Every priest's major responsibilities are: Growing in his or her relationship with God, and making Him known to others.

Notice there are four elements in this Wheel illustration:

- The Vertical Spokes—the *Great Commandment*
- The Horizontal Spokes—the *Great Commission*
- The Hub—the *Great Commander (Jesus) and Great Empowerment (Holy Spirit)*
- The Rim—the *Great Commitment*

In the remainder of this chapter, we will examine the vertical and horizontal dimensions of the Wheel: The Great Commandment and the Great Commission. In Chapter 3, we will conclude the study of this illustration, focusing on the Hub—the source of power in a believer's life—and the Rim—the commitment required to fully function as God's priest in the world.

Training in the Great Commandment

Notice the Wheel has two dimensions. They complement each other. That is to say, we demonstrate our love for God in the Great Commandment (the vertical spoke) through our obedience to the Great Commission (the horizontal spoke). The true fulfillment of our priestly identity is to obey both commandments outlined in Matthew 22:37-40: To love God, and to love your neighbors. John reminds us that we demonstrate love for God by keeping His commandments.

> *He who has My commandments and keeps them, it is he who loves Me. And he who loves Me will be loved by My Father, and I will love him and manifest Myself to him.*
> *John 14:21*

In John chapter 21 Jesus says to Peter, "Do you love me?" When Peter answers in the affirmative, Jesus replies, "Feed my sheep." We therefore demonstrate our love ***vertically*** in a ***horizontal*** fashion. Love is incomplete unless it includes the dimension of reaching out to those around us through evangelism and discipleship. This gives us a clear picture of how a New Testament believer is to function as a priest.

Jesus walked in perfect obedience to the commandments of God. Since He had no agenda of His own, He could walk in perfect harmony with His Father—neither getting ahead nor falling behind. The Scriptures record that He only did what His Father told Him to do. The *hallmark* of Jesus' training was waiting on the Father—obediently doing and saying only what He was commanded.

> *For I have come down from heaven, not to do My own will, but the will of Him who sent Me.*
> *John 6:38*

> *Then Jesus said to them, "When you lift up the Son of Man, then you will know that I am He, and that I do nothing of Myself; but as My Father taught Me, I speak these things."*
> *John 8:28*

How was He able to maintain His vision and keep His life in such perfect balance? It was His careful communication with the Father as commanded by the **Shema** (see below) that kept Him in harmony with God's perfect will for Him. Mark gives us the key to this in his Gospel.

> *Now in the morning, having risen a long while before daylight, He went out and departed to a solitary place; and there He prayed.*
> *Mark 1:35*

The Word of God

The key to the effectiveness of Jesus' earthly ministry was His flawless command of Scripture. It is in the pages of His Word that God lays out for us both **His will** and **His purpose** for our lives. The Word can guide us during our short earthly sojourn.

That is why the **Shema**, the central tenet of Judaism, commands us to write the Word of God upon our hearts. It alone can tell us our eternal purpose. It answers the three great questions of life: **Who** am I?, **Why** am I here?, and **What** am I to do while I am here? In rising before daybreak to meet with His Father, Jesus showed us this command in action.

> *"Hear, O Israel: The Lord our God, the Lord is one! You shall love the Lord your God with all your heart, with all your soul, and with all your might. And these words which I command you today shall be in your heart; you shall teach them diligently to your children, and shall talk of them when you sit in your house, when you walk by the way, when you lie down, and when you rise up. You shall bind them as a sign on your hand, and they shall be as frontlets between your eyes. You shall write them on the doorposts of your house and on your gates."*
>
> *Deuteronomy 6:4-9*

Jesus spent a great deal of time with His Father, allowing the Word to minister to Him. As He reviewed the commandments, He allowed the Spirit of God to guide His meditation, writing the words of the prophets upon His heart. Obedience to God's commandments allowed the Savior to declare with certainty, "I only speak what God has given me to speak."

> *Then Jesus said to them, "When you lift up the Son of Man, then you will know that I am He, and that I do nothing of Myself; but as my Father taught Me, I speak these things."*
>
> *John 8:28*

pR^{the}īestHOOD
^{of}eveRy BeLieveR

Jesus set the pace by demonstrating the need to continue in the Word of God on a regular basis. Intake of the Word of God is one of the key disciplines in the life of a true discipling priest. Reading, studying, memorizing and allowing God's Spirit to guide our meditation will equip us to help others hear God's voice and teach them how to discern His will.

Where the vertical spokes of the Wheel are concerned, the Word is of paramount importance in deepening our love relationship with God. The Apostle Paul reminds us in II Timothy 3:16 that all Scriptures are God-breathed and that they accomplish four very important things for a disciple/priest:

- **Doctrine**—describes the proper path to walk
- **Reproof**—describes where we may have strayed from the path
- **Correction**—describes how to get back on the path
- **Instruction**—describes how to stay on the correct path

> *All Scripture is given by inspiration of God, and is profitable for doctrine, for reproof, for correction, for instruction in righteousness.*
> *II Timothy 3:16*

Because Jesus was such a ***master*** of the Word, He was able to defeat Satan by reciting Scripture (Matthew 4). Each of His replies to Satan during His temptation is prefaced by the words, ***"It is written."*** He was furthermore able to show people that John the Baptist was the Elijah foretold in Malachi's prophecy. When He was accused of breaking the Sabbath by healing and doing good, He turned to Scripture to validate the error of the Pharisees. At the Passover celebration in the upper room, Jesus deftly correlated His Last Supper with the institution of the New

Covenant in Jeremiah 31:31-34. On the Cross Jesus prayed the words of Psalm 22:1—"My God, My God, why hast Thou forsaken Me?" From start to finish the Scriptures were the very breath of Jesus' life and ministry.

Prayer

Another prominent element of Jesus' life and ministry was His devotion to prayer. In Luke's Gospel we learn of the disciples' fascination with His desire and ability to communicate or dialogue continually with His Father. They often saw Him slipping away for these engaging conversations. What we know about Jesus' practices and teachings on the subject of prayer we learn from His disciples. They prayed with Him, and even recorded for us some of His prayers. In fact, the one thing we know the disciples specifically asked Jesus to teach them was how to pray.

> *And it came to pass, as He was praying in a certain place, when He ceased, that one of His disciples said to Him, "Lord teach us to pray, as John also taught his disciples."*
> *Luke 11:1*

One of the most moving of all the prayers of our Messiah was His high priestly prayer, which He prayed for His disciples in the Garden of Gethsemane just prior to His arrest and subsequent crucifixion. John recorded that prayer for us in great detail in John 17:1-26.

Christ furthermore gave the disciples a model prayer that addresses nine things we should consider when we pray. This is most often referred to as The Lord's Prayer. It is recorded in the Gospels by both Matthew and Luke. This prayer has been recited by God's people for centuries, and continues to guide the prayers of disciples throughout the world:

> *In this manner, therefore, pray:*
> *Our Father in heaven,*
> *Hallowed be Your name.*
> *Your kingdom come.*
> *Your will be done*
> *On earth as it is in heaven.*
> *Give us this day our daily bread.*
> *And forgive us our debts,*
> *As we forgive our debtors.*
> *And do not lead us into temptation,*
> *But deliver us from the evil one.*
> *For Yours is the kingdom and the power*
> *And the glory forever. Amen.*
> *Matthew 6:9-13*

Observe in this passage nine elements or aspects of prayer. They transcend casual recitation and become a guide to the believer/priest as he seeks to develop his own prayer life and teaches others to pray:

- Address God as Father
- Honor the Name of God
- Pray in the Kingdom
- Pray and live out His will
- Pray for daily needs
- Pray with a forgiving spirit
- Pray against temptation
- Pray for deliverance
- Acknowledge God's sovereignty

As Jesus heard the Old Testament read by the Rabbis in the Synagogue, His mind was saturated by the prayers of the Old Testament patriarchs and psalmists like David, each of whom were great men of prayer. New Testament priests ought to carefully study these same prayers, and Jesus' prayers, which yield guidance in petitioning God for personal needs and intercession for the needs of others. The keys to Jesus' growing relationship with His Father were the **Word** and **Prayer**. Humanly speaking, these account for His spotless and sinless life. It was His obedience to God's directives that made these two activities such a natural part of His life, and He naturally reproduced these priestly activities in the lives of the Twelve whom He trained.

Training in the Great Commission

We have examined the first of the two commandments in Matthew 22—the Great Commandment—and the important part it played in the life of the Master.

However, Jesus said that *everything that God wants and expects hangs on **two commands***. The first is the **vertical command**, focused on personal growth and love for God, and expressed through our intimate worship, intercession and reflection on Holy Scripture. The second commandment is **horizontal**. Jesus trains the Twelve to present the Kingdom of God to people who do not yet know Him. This is commonly referred to as *evangelism*. He further taught them how to train those who had come to know God but who had not grown in their relationship with Him. *Discipleship* involves helping people understand *Who* they are, *Why* they are here, and *What* they are to be doing. Biblical discipleship must balance the Great Commandment with the Great Commission— the vertical spokes with the horizontal spokes.

Simply put, it involves **winning** lost people and then **discipling** them. To bring them to full maturity as believers and priests, new disciples must be trained or mentored, and then sent out, just as the Lord Jesus sent out the Twelve.

Evangelism

Matthew records the very first words of Jesus' ministry: "Repent, for the Kingdom of God is at hand." Jesus was calling His generation to repentance and faith. Some of those to whom He preached were religious people, who had lost sight of the need for a personal relationship with God in their legalistic devotion to the letter of the law. The Rabbis taught people to keep 613 laws, which, of course, they were incapable of doing. Their religion required them to attend services, pay tithes and observe festivals and feasts. They lived in anticipation of a Savior, but had little idea what it would mean to know Him personally.

At Mt. Sinai, their fathers had rejected God's plan for them to become a nation of priests, choosing instead to follow a system of their own devising. Their creedal system had brought them full circle—back into the same bondage God had sought to deliver them from 1500 years earlier! Their religious observances failed to answer the most fundamental questions of all: **Who** they were, **Why** they were here and **What** they were supposed to be doing.

The disciples learned how to do evangelism (the horizontal spoke or the second Commandment) by watching Jesus deal with religious people. A part of their priestly training was to help people restore a proper relationship with the Father. Jesus promised the Twelve that He would make them fishers of men. He did this intentionally by allowing them to watch HIM fish!

*And He said to them, "Follow Me, and I will make you
fishers of men."*
                                    Matthew 4:19

Sometimes He evangelized the lost in the disciples' absence, and
this too served to set an example. The story recorded in John
4—the woman at the well—is a case in point. John documented
in detail a dialogue between Jesus and a woman in the town
of Samaria. Because she placed her trust in the Messiah, the
entire city was drawn to the Lord. Jesus not only produced a
convert, but an evangelist—a priest(ess) who immediately
became a reproducing disciple!

What are the fundamental principles these early disciple/priests
exemplified to others? The Gospel is the Good News, which sets
people free from the bondage of sin and rote religious practice.
This message is so clear and simple anyone can understand it
and share it with others. It is outlined in Scripture and consists
of at least these four truths:

- Everyone has sinned.
- There is a penalty for sin.
- Sin was paid for by Christ's death.
- One must receive Christ's sacrifice as payment for sin.

There are many ways to share the Good News of the Gospel with
others. Romans 6:23 is perhaps the most concise statement of
this eternal truth:

> *For the wages of sin is death, but the gift of God is
> eternal life in Christ Jesus our Lord.*
>   *Romans 6:23*

PRiesTHOOD
ᵒᶠevery BeLieveR

The Twelve keenly observed Jesus demonstrating His love for people as He drew them to Himself in various situations. After they had been sufficiently trained, Christ sent this band of brothers out in pairs to do what they had been taught.

So they went out and preached that people should repent.
Mark 6:12

Discipling

Once people come to Christ, we have the responsibility to help them understand that they were not called to practice a religion, but to develop an *intimate relationship* with God (the Great Commandment). New believers should be taught to apply the principles of the **Shema** to their lives, as did Jesus and His disciples. Reading, studying and memorizing the Word of God, praying and understanding the role of the Holy Spirit Who guides our meditation—all these things are foundational to the growth of new believers. Devotional practices are the cornerstone of a believer's spiritual development. They are the substance of the first **commandment** which is no mere **suggestion**. Obedience will bring freedom, joy and purpose, and will answer the questions of **Who** we are, **Why** we are here, and **What** we are to be doing. Disobedience only returns us to the bondage from which Jesus came to set us free. Obedience will assure that a convert becomes a maturing disciple/priest.

Jesus trained His men for their priestly functions in the **midst** of ministry, not in *classroom* conditions. These followers of the Savior saw *firsthand* how He reached out to people in almost every conceivable circumstance of life.

The disciples observed Jesus Christ as He made the blind to see, the lame to walk, and the deaf to hear. Lepers were healed, demons were cast out and the dead were raised to life. There was no human suffering that Jesus could not heal. Wherever and to whomever it was needed, our Savior brought comfort, peace and hope. These first followers saw the Father give Him power even over the elements of nature when He calmed a raging storm, walked on water, and fed people from nothing. They further saw God give Him insight and wisdom to deal with religious leaders who hated Him and wanted to kill Him. They were given detailed instructions addressing every situation they would encounter when they were sent out to minister. Jesus knew they would be successful because He had thoroughly trained them, and had lived and traveled with them for nearly two years. As we have noted, they were not merely given classroom principles to follow, but real life, on-the-job applications.

Sending

When the Twelve were trained and ready to put into practice what they had learned, Jesus sent them out two-by-two. They were given detailed instructions and permitted to begin their public ministry. There is no record of the *length* of this internship, but the *outcome* is recounted in Scripture, when the newly ordained priests returned to report the success of their mission to Jesus. They were rejoicing, for they had experienced the Father using them in amazing ways. The things Jesus taught them bore fruit in their ministries. They shared how the ministry of repentance had caused many to return to the Father. God authenticated their calling by casting demons out of people who were possessed by the powers of darkness. They watched God heal all manner of sickness as they prayed and anointed the sick with oil.

> *So they went out and preached that people should*
> *repent. And they cast out many demons, and anointed*
> *with oil many who were sick, and healed them.*
> *Mark 6:12,13*

Jesus had created a model for training disciples who understood their priestly calling. The disciples followed His model as they demonstrated their ability to represent God to their own nation. Jesus put the finishing touches on their training during His triumphal entry into Jerusalem. He answered their questions about end-time events in His Mount Olivet discourse. He taught them about the ministry of the Holy Spirit at the Passover meal, and although they witnessed His arrest and crucifixion with grief and incomprehension, He was able to clarify many things to them during the 40 days after His resurrection and before His ascension. Just before He ascended to heaven, the apostle/priests were given their final marching orders for the discipling of the nations.

This chapter has been devoted to an inspection of the vertical and horizontal dimensions of our relationships with God and other people. We have represented those relationships with the Wheel illustration. In chapter 3, we will continue examining the Wheel: The Rim, our commitment, and the Hub, our empowerment through the Holy Spirit.

3

Priesthood Empowerment

The Great Empowerment

In this chapter, which continues the discussion from Chapter 2, we will focus again on the Wheel illustration. In the last chapter we concentrated on the *vertical* and *horizontal* spokes which represent the Two Great Commandments in the Law given in Matthew 22:

- **The Great Commandment** ➤ Love God
- **The Great Commission** ➤ Love Your Neighbor

The remainder of the illustration addresses our response to these commands: *We need to avail ourselves of the power the Father has provided in order to obey His directives (the Hub) and we need to make a commitment to them (the Rim).*

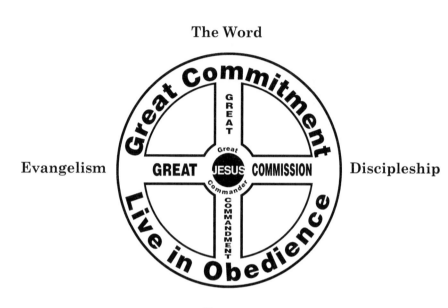

The Word

Evangelism · Discipleship

Prayer

Jesus, the Great Commander, is illustrated as the very center of the believer's life. It is He Who has given us the Great Commandments in the Law, and it is He Who then makes provision for us to fulfill His commands. As the Father sent the Son, the Son sends us, but first He baptizes us with His Spirit.

The Promise of Empowerment

The last thing Jesus told His disciples to do was to *remain in Jerusalem until they were empowered by the Holy Spirit,* Who was to be given them in a matter of days. John the Baptist had prophesied this event some three and a half years earlier when he baptized Jesus:

*I indeed baptized you with water, but He will baptize
you with the Holy Spirit.*

Mark 1:8

In three and a half years of ministry, Jesus only made reference
to the Holy Spirit on four occasions in His teachings:

- He taught against blaspheming the Holy Spirit.
  (Matthew 12:31)
- He quoted King David's reference to the Holy Spirit.
  (Mark 12:36)
- He said the Holy Spirit is a gift the Father will give
  to His children. (Luke 11:13)
- He said that the Holy Spirit would teach us what
  to say in "that hour". (Luke 12:12)

At the Last Supper, Jesus told His men of His impending death.
He promised them that He would be with them, and that they
would not be left alone. In John 14-16, the ministry of the Holy
Spirit is outlined. Jesus gave His followers a special filling of
the Spirit until He was ready for them to receive the Spirit,
Who would then remain with them permanently. He said it was
expedient for Him to depart that He might send the Holy Spirit
to fill them, minister to them and empower them to live Godly
lives and to minister to others—their priestly function of winning
and discipling the nations.

In the book of Acts, just before Jesus ascended into Heaven, He
gave this promise to His disciples:

*But you shall receive power when the Holy Spirit has
come upon you...*

Acts 1:8

That same power, active in Jesus' life from conception to resurrection, then became available to the Eleven and is now accessible to every believer until Jesus returns. When filled with His Spirit, we are given power over Satan and all the forces of hell and darkness. ***We must minister not in the power of our flesh, but in the power of the Third Person of the Trinity.*** Just as Jesus was victorious in the Spirit, we also can experience victory through the Spirit.

Jesus' Empowerment

The Holy Spirit was a powerful agent at work in the life and ministry of Jesus Christ. Jesus did nothing that He did not hear His Father tell Him to do, and He only spoke what He heard the Father speak. When He acted, He depended on the power of the Holy Spirit to accomplish the work the Father had given Him to do. The Gospel writers record many occasions of the Spirit's activity in His life:

- **Jesus was conceived by the Holy Spirit.**

    And the angel answered and said to her, "The Holy Spirit will come upon you, and the power of the Highest will overshadow you, therefore also, that Holy One who is born will be called the Son of God."
    Luke 1:35

- **The Holy Spirit descended upon Jesus**

    When He had been baptized, Jesus came up immediately from the water; And behold, the heavens were opened to him, and He saw the Spirit of God descending like a dove and alighting upon Him.
    Matthew 3:16

- **Jesus was filled with the Spirit and led by the Spirit to the wilderness to be tempted.**

  Then Jesus, being filled with the Holy Spirit, returned from the Jordan and was led by the Spirit into the wilderness.

  Luke 4:1

- **Jesus was sealed by the Spirit.**

  Do not labor for the food which perishes, but for the food which endures to everlasting life, which the Son of Man will give you, because God the Father has set His seal on Him.

  John 6:27

- **Jesus was anointed by the Spirit.**

  The Spirit of the LORD is upon Me, because He has anointed Me to preach the gospel to the poor; He has sent Me to heal the brokenhearted, to proclaim liberty to the captives and recovery of sight to the blind, to set at liberty those who are oppressed; to proclaim the acceptable year of the LORD.

  Luke 4:18,19

- **Jesus cast out demons by the Spirit.**

  "But if I cast out demons by the Spirit of God, surely the kingdom of God has come upon you."

  Matthew 12:28

- **Jesus rejoiced in the Spirit.**

  In that hour Jesus rejoiced in the Spirit and said, "I thank You, Father, Lord of heaven and earth, that you have hidden these things from the wise and prudent and revealed them to babes. Even so, Father, for so it seemed good in Your sight."

  Luke 10:21

- **Jesus offered Himself up through the Spirit.**

  How much more shall the blood of Christ, who through the eternal Spirit offered Himself without spot to God, cleanse your conscience from dead works to serve the living God?

  Hebrews 9:14

- **Jesus was raised from the dead by the Spirit.**

  ...concerning His Son Jesus Christ our Lord, who was born of the seed of David according to the flesh, and declared to be the Son of God with power according to the Spirit of holiness, by the resurrection from the dead.

  Romans 1:3.4

- **Jesus gave commands to His disciples by the Spirit.**

  ...until the day in which He was taken up, after He through the Holy Spirit had given commandments to the apostles whom He had chosen, to whom He also presented Himself alive after His suffering by many infallible proofs, being seen by them during forty days and speaking of the things pertaining to the kingdom of God.

  Acts 1:2,3

Our Empowerment

As noted, if Jesus depended on the Holy Spirit, so must we. The Spirit is given to empower us in our walk with God and in the performance of our priestly functions. Every person has a throne in his life and someone is ruling from that throne. Only when a person has totally surrendered his life to Christ does the Holy Spirit rule his life from that throne. The Bible speaks about three kinds of people: The Natural, the Carnal, and the Spiritual.

We might illustrate them in this way:

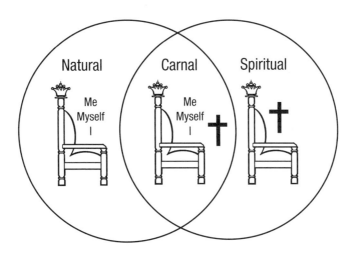

Natural   Carnal   Spiritual

Me Myself I   Me Myself I

Chair Illustration

The Natural Man

The Bible describes the Natural Man as unable to receive the things of God. He may know about God intellectually, but has never entered into a personal relationship with Him. The Natural

Man sits on the throne of own his life. Although Satan rules and controls him, he believes himself the master. All mankind is born in this condition.

> *But the natural man does not receive the things of the Spirit of God, for they are foolishness to him; nor can he know them, because they are spiritually discerned.*
> *I Corinthians 2:14*

The Carnal Man

The believer begins his new life as a spiritual man. But without the disciplines of the Christian life and a growing intimacy with Christ—he slides all too easily into the center chair of carnality. The Carnal Man knows the Lord, but is still trying to govern his own life. He wants Jesus to be the co-pilot but not the Lord of his life. **One of the first things the Holy Spirit teaches a new believer/priest is that Jesus is Lord, not just Savior.** The Carnal Man makes choices based upon his old sinful nature and ends up doing the very things from which God is trying to deliver him. The decisions he makes are contrary to God's will.

> *And I, brethren, could not speak to you as to spiritual people but as to carnal, as to babes in Christ. I fed you with milk and not with solid food; for until now you were not able to receive it, and even now you are still not able; for you are still carnal. For where there are envy, strife, and divisions among you, are you not carnal and behaving like mere men? For when one says, "I am of Paul," and another, "I am of Apollos," are you not carnal?*
> *I Corinthians 3:1-4*

The Spiritual Man

The Spiritual Man, in observing the **Shema**, is transformed by the Word of God, and begins to reflect the very mind of Christ. He learns to allow the Holy Spirit to totally control the innermost parts of his life, where the mind, the will and the emotions—the decision-making processes—operate. The Scriptures teach that we are spirit/soul/body. When a man is born again, the Holy Spirit comes to live within his spirit, and directs him into God's perfect will for his life. The new believer dies to himself, so that God is able to live His life through him. Paul said it this way:

I have been crucified with Christ; it is no longer I who live, but Christ lives in me; and the life which I now live in the flesh I live by faith in the Son of God, who loved me and gave Himself for me.
Galatians 2:20

Each person is born a Natural Man. When spiritual re-birth occurs, an amazing alteration takes place. The Bible says:

He has delivered us from the domain of darkness and transferred us to the kingdom of his beloved Son.
Colossians 1:13 ESV

In terms of the Chair Illustration above, we jump from the Natural chair to the Spiritual chair—a mid-air transformation! We become **spiritual children of God**. To understand this more fully, consider that all men are created as tripartite beings: Spirit, soul and body (just as God is a triune being). We could illustrate this using the following diagram:

p̲r̲ī̲e̲s̲t̲ʰᵉhOOD
ᵒᶠeveRy BeLieveR

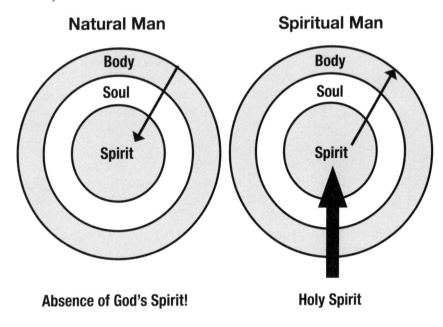

Natural Man

Body

Soul

Spirit

Absence of God's Spirit!

Spiritual Man

Body

Soul

Spirit

Holy Spirit

Now may the God of peace Himself sanctify you completely; and may your whole **spirit**, **soul**, *and* **body** *be preserved blameless at the coming of our Lord Jesus Christ.*

I Thessalonians 5:23

In these two illustrations, the circles represent the three parts of our being referenced by Paul in the passage above: ***spirit, soul, and body***. At physical birth, our bodies and souls become alive, but our spirits are dead. At re-birth, our spirits are made alive when God's Spirit comes to indwell us. The Natural Man continues with a dead spirit because he has not yet experienced spiritual re-birth in Christ and the subsequent filling of God's Holy Spirit.

A major contrast between the Natural and Spiritual is found in the way people live their lives and make decisions. The Natural Man lives life from the *outside in*—meaning from the external to the internal. Outward circumstances and worldly philosophies influence his soul; thus, his mind, will and emotions are misguided. His decision-making processes are often in error, because he makes no allowance for the God who created him. He has no Holy Spirit to guide his thinking and the unholy spirit (Satan) cleverly entangles him in temporal matters.

The Spiritual Man, by contrast, lives his life from the inside out—meaning from the internal to the external. The Spirit of God controls his soul and body, allowing him to live out the principles of the **Shema**. Jesus taught His disciples to live in this way, and we as New Testament priests are to do the same, helping those we disciple avoid the trap of carnality.

The only way a born-again believer can escape becoming a Carnal Man is to die to the old, Natural Man, and allow the new Spiritual Man to control his life. Without the Word, prayer and obedience to God's commandments, a Spiritual Man easily slides to the middle chair of carnality. How does one escape from this carnality? The same way one is re-born in the beginning: **Confession, repentance and a change of heart**. Immediately, God's grace and mercy come to bear on the wandering soul, and that prodigal son is restored to fellowship as a Spiritual Man.

Fulfillment of Our Empowerment

Ten days after Jesus ascended to Heaven, at the Feast of Pentecost, the Holy Spirit of God was poured out powerfully upon the eleven disciples as well as on 120 souls in an upper room in Jerusalem. Within 50 years these early Christians had turned the world upside down by ministering in the Spirit's power! As we have seen, today that same Spirit comes to take up residence in our lives. He is the One who brings transformation, and makes us ready to become fishers of men and makers of disciples. He is the key to our sanctification and maturity. Fruit will accrue to New Testament priests as we learn to minister in the power of the Holy Spirit rather than in the flesh.

In our Wheel Illustration, power to the Rim is transmitted from the Hub through the spokes. The power of the Holy Spirit is the driving agent. It is He who enables the believer to make a commitment to God's plan for the ages: Reaching every tongue, tribe and nation with the Good News of Salvation. It is He who restores God's Law of First Intent—*The Priesthood of Every Believer.*

The Great Commitment

Three Thousand Converted

Jesus baptized the disciples with His Spirit just as John had prophesied. They began to speak and minister to the crowd that had formed. Peter's sermon caused some 3,000 souls to turn to Christ and be baptized.

> *Then those who gladly received his word were baptized; and that day about three thousand souls were added to them.*
>
> *Acts 2:41*

Three Thousand Established

The Apostles at once began to confirm and establish the 3,000 converts in their newfound faith by teaching them all that Jesus had commanded them. This, along with prayer, fellowship and the Lord's Supper, helped to make the **Shema** a reality and accelerated the transformation of the new converts into true disciples.

> *And they continued steadfastly in the apostles' doctrine and fellowship, in the breaking of bread, and in prayers.*
> *Acts 2:42*

Converts Were Added Daily

The disciples continued to walk with God and to preach repentance to all who would listen. Their joy and worship, combined with God's authentication of their ministry through signs and wonders, caused many to be added to the fellowship of believers daily.

> *Praising God and having favor with the people. And the Lord added to the church daily those who were being saved.*
> *Acts 2:47*

Disciples Were Multiplied

By chapter 6 of Acts, these early disciples were being taught not only to have a personal, vertical relationship with God, but also to win and establish others—balancing the Great Commandment with the Great Commission. The result was the amazing phenomenon of multiplication. They no longer simply added converts, but focused on making and multiplying disciples.

> *Now in those days when the number of disciples was multiplying...*
> *Acts 6:1*

p*the*riesthood
*of*every Believer

Disciples Were Taught to be Priests

A part of the training of the early church had to do with what we have referred to as the Law of First Intent, so there was clear teaching on each believer's identity. Even great numbers of the Levitical priesthood became obedient to their true calling, and joined the disciples in teaching what Jesus had taught them, thereby multiplying the **true priesthood**.

> *And the word of God spread, and the number of disciples multiplied greatly in Jerusalem, and a great many of the priests were obedient to the faith.*
> *Acts 6:7*

Churches Were Multiplied in Judea, Samaria, Galilee and Beyond

Chapter 9 of the book of Acts documents that the ministry reached out to many surrounding regions. People were meeting together and churches were being formed. In this chapter we learn of a church in Damascus, one that Saul (who after his conversion was renamed Paul) sought to persecute. This persecution brought growth everywhere.

> *Then the churches throughout all Judea, Galilee, and Samaria had peace and were edified. And walking in the fear of the Lord and in the comfort of the Holy Spirit, they were multiplied.*
> *Acts 9:31*

> *Now those who were scattered after the persecution that arose over Stephen traveled as far as Phoenicia, Cyprus, and Antioch, preaching the word to no one but*

the Jews only. But some of them were men from Cyprus and Cyrene, who when they had come to Antioch, spoke to the Hellenists, preaching the Lord Jesus. And the hand of the Lord was with them, and a great number believed and turned to the Lord.

Acts 11:19-21

The Church Reaches Out to the Gentiles

God directed Peter to reach out to the Gentile world through Cornelius, fulfilling the promise that Abraham was to be a blessing to the whole world and not just to the nation of Israel.

About the ninth hour of the day he saw clearly in a vision an angel of God coming in and saying to him, "Cornelius!" And when he observed him, he was afraid, and said, "What is it, Lord?" So he said to him, "Your prayers and your alms have come up for a memorial before God. "Now send men to Joppa and send for Simon whose surname is Peter."

Acts 10:3-5

Church Began Sending Missionaries

Paul and Barnabas were sent out as missionaries in obedience to the Holy Spirit's direction, and this opened the door for the church to begin sending other missionaries throughout the Mediterranean basin.

Now in the church that was at Antioch there were certain prophets and teachers; Barnabas, Simeon who was called Niger, Luscius of Cyrene, Manaen who had been brought up with Herod the tetrarch,

> *and Saul. As they ministered to the Lord and fasted,*
> *the Holy Spirit said, "Now separate to Me Barnabas*
> *and Saul for the work to which I have called them."*
> *Then, having fasted and prayed, and laid hands on*
> *them, they sent them away.*
>
> *Acts 13:1-3*

The World Was Turned Upside Down

By the time Paul embarked on his second missionary journey, the charge brought against him and his team in Thessalonica was, *"The world is being turned upside down,"* indicating once again the explosive growth of the early church. The early missionaries, disciples who understood their priestly calling, took seriously their responsibility to take the message of the Gospel to the world!

> *But when they did not find them, they dragged Jason*
> *and some brethren to the rulers of the city, crying out,*
> *"These who have turned the world upside down have*
> *come here too."*
>
> *Acts 17:6*

Disciples Trained the Gentiles in Their Priestly Function

Paul and his team trained the Gentiles in their priestly mission so they were equipped to win and disciple others. The Thessalonians were responsible for reaching the areas of Macedonia and Achaia.

> *For our gospel did not come to you in word only, but*
> *also in power, and in the Holy Spirit and in much*
> *assurance, as you know what kind of men we were*
> *among you for your sake. And you became followers*
> *of us and of the Lord, having received the word in*

much affliction, with joy of the Holy Spirit, so that
you became examples to all in Macedonia and Achaia
who believe. For from you the word of the Lord has
sounded forth, not only in Macedonia and Achaia,
but also in every place. Your faith toward God has
gone out, so that we do not need to say anything. For
they themselves declare concerning us what manner of
entry we had to you, and how you turned to God from
idols to serve the living and true God, and to wait for
His Son from heaven, Whom He raised from the dead,
even Jesus who delivers us from the wrath to come.
I Thessalonians 1:5-10

Gospel Spread to the Entire World

When Paul wrote his letter to the Colossian church some 35
years after the death of Christ, the Gospel had gone out to the
entire known world—every creature had heard!

Because of the hope which is laid up for you in heaven,
of which you heard before in the word of the truth of
*the gospel, which has come to you, as it has also in **all***
***the world**, and is bringing forth fruit, as it is also*
among you since the day you heard and knew the grace
of God in truth.
Colossians 1:5,6

If indeed you continue in the faith, grounded and
steadfast, and are not moved away from the hope of
*the gospel which you heard, **which was preached***
***to every creature under heaven**, of which I, Paul*
became a minister.
Colossians 1:23

pRÏest^{the}HOOD
^{of}eveRy BeLÏeveR

Disciples Followed Jesus' Model of Training

Like Jesus, Paul had a band of men who traveled with him. Following the model of his leader, Paul trained his band of brothers in the midst of the battle, helping them to understand the priestly duties to which all followers of the Messiah are called.

> *And Sopater of Berea accompanied him to Asia—also Aristarchus and Secundus of the Thessalonians, and Gaius of Derbe, and Timothy, and Tychicus and Trophimus of Asia.*
>
> Acts 20:4

Jesus' Ministry Produced a Winning Combination

- **Disciples who knew *Who* they were**

> *You did not choose Me, but I chose you and appointed you that you should go and bear fruit, and that your fruit should remain, that whatever you ask the Father in My name He may give you.*
>
> John 15:16

- **Disciples who knew *Why* they were here**

> *And He Himself gave some to be apostles, some prophets, some evangelists, and some pastors and teachers, for the equipping of the saints for the work of ministry, for the edifying of the body of Christ.*
>
> Ephesians 4:11,12

- **Disciples who knew *What* they were to be doing**

  Then Jesus came and spoke to them, saying, "All authority has been given to Me in heaven and on earth. Go therefore and make disciples of all the nations, baptizing them in the name of the Father and of the Son and of the Holy Spirit..."
  Matthew 28:18-20

- **Disciples who were carefully trained to do the ministry**

  So they went out and preached that people should repent. And they cast out many demons, and anointed with oil many who were sick, and healed them.
  Mark 6:12,13

- **Disciples who were empowered by the Holy Spirit**

  And they were all filled with the Holy Spirit and began to speak with other tongues, as the Spirit gave them utterance.
  Acts 2:4

- **Disciples who were willing to die for the objective**

  And they cast him out of the city and stoned him. And the witnesses laid down their clothes at the feet of a young man named Saul. And they stoned Stephen as he was calling on God and saying, "Lord Jesus, receive my spirit."
  Acts 7:58,59

This early explosive growth of the church was a direct result of obedience to God's Law of First Intent—a return to the prominent role of individuals taking their place in God's army by becoming His instruments of redemption in the world. Any man at any time was again the operative principle, and the focus was not on a professional priesthood. In fact, the *Levitical priests* were quite disconcerted by the behavior of these early ***believer/priests,*** assuming their motives and actions ran contrary to the Law and Commandments.

In Chapter 4, we will confront the unfortunate regression of the people of God to a way of life dominated by the Old Testament model of a professional priesthood.

4

The Priesthood Modified

Modification Brought Disaster

In the previous chapter, we celebrated the incredible growth of the early church in the opening pages of the New Testament. After the life, ministry, death and resurrection of Jesus Christ, those who had walked with the Master during His time on earth began to take seriously His call to action. They grasped the seriousness of the call to become *believer/priests*, and began to multiply ministry throughout Israel and the surrounding Gentile nations.

The Law of First Intent had taken root again, but not for long. The early New Testament church leaders altered God's expansion plan just as Israel's leaders had in the Old Testament. In each case, the results were calamitous.

Consider these two verses that are pertinent to this study:

There is a way that seems right to a man, but its end is the way of death.

Proverbs 14:12

"For My thoughts are not your thoughts, nor are your ways My ways," says the Lord. "For as the heavens are higher than the earth, so are My ways higher than your ways, and My thoughts than your thoughts."

Isaiah 55:8,9

When leaders in the Old and New Testaments altered God's perfect plan, they could not have anticipated the consequences their actions would have or the way those consequences would carry down through the centuries. Today, we suffer from their misguided choices.

How the Modification Occurred

There are four words that are key to this modification in the New Testament vocabulary:

Laikos—This is a secular Greek term that describes someone who is uneducated, or who knows little about the subject under consideration. The Greeks call this person a *layman*. We call this term 'secular' because ***the word doesn't appear anywhere in the New Testament***. The New Testament knows nothing about a *laity* because the New Testament is built on the priesthood of every believer.

Laos—This is a New Testament word and is used over 135 times. It means *people*, or the *people of God*. There are many nouns in the New Testament that refer to **laos**. They include believer, Christian, disciple, or saint. Laos denotes a peer relationship and does not refer to rank or distinction, since all are the people of God.

Kleros—This is another New Testament word that means a *lot*, *portion*, or *part*. Both **laos** and **kleros** apply to people—in this case a ***group*** of people. Because of the sound and spelling of the word, it was easy to assume **kleros** meant *clergy* and denoted an elite group. However, there is no indication that the church of the first century knew anything about distinct classes of clergy and laity. In the New Testament church *every* believer was part of the **laos**—the people of God—as well as the **kleros**, whose part was to serve as priests of God. These terms designate a relationship between peers that unites all children of God.

Clerus—This is another secular word, since it also ***does not appear anywhere in the New Testament***. It means a person who holds an *ecclesiastical office,* and it is the word we translate as *clergy*. It emphasizes ***position*** or status, rather than ***function***. It draws a distinction between an educated clergy and an uneducated laity, but every Biblical adjective that is used in the New Testament contradicts such a distinction. The New Testament focuses on our peer relationships as members of the Body of Christ. Dictionaries provide us the meanings of words so that we may clearly understand an author's intent. *When we modify and assign new meanings to words to suit our own ends, we court disaster.* This revision is what happened in the early church. James Garlow, in his excellent book *Partners in Ministry*, has outlined this tragic modification. His detailed study provides great insight into the historical regression of God's great Plan of the Ages.[1]

---

[1] James Garlow, *Partners in Ministry*, © 1998 Beacon Hill Press, Kansas City.

Clement of Rome

At the end of the first century, Clement of Rome, one of the early church fathers, introduced the word *layman* (laikos) into the vocabulary of the early church. He elevated the church leaders' *functional* role into a *positional* one. This created a hierarchy that allowed the clergy/laity structure to arise. It is unclear whether Clement intended to move the structure of the church back to the historic, Old Testament Levitical model of ministry.

It is interesting to note that the book of Revelation is written at this same time. The Apostle John may have foreseen this error and tried to head it off. In John's Gospel, he opens with a clear statement dealing with the deity of Jesus Christ, who was God incarnate. In Revelation, John gives us an equally distinct statement of Jesus' intention that we are to be priests:

> *And from Jesus Christ, the faithful witness, the firstborn from the dead, and the ruler over the kings of the earth. To Him who loved us and washed us from our sins in His own blood, and has made us **kings** and **priests** to His God and Father, to Him be glory and Dominion forever and ever. Amen.*
>
> *Revelation 1:5,6*

If this truly was John's intent, it was soon lost, as *status* and *position* became paramount and *function* became secondary.

Origen

A hundred years later, Origen, another early church father, began to refer to a class of **kleros**, who held ecclesiastical offices. These leaders were endowed with privileges and status, and began to function as the **clerus** or clergy. Their elevated position focused on *who they were*. This became more important than *what they were to do* and their functional role of making disciples who understood their priestly responsibilities. This elite group of men lost sight of the Law of First Intent and the objective of training priests to represent God to the pagan nations of the earth.

Council of Nicea

In A.D. 325, one of the most important meetings held by the early church took place. The Council of Nicea grappled with the early writing and canonizing of a text that would become our Bible. Although most of what the council accomplished was necessary and positive, they unfortunately defined the church as a clerical order, thus widening the gap between clergy and laity.

Jerome

In A.D. 340, Jerome, a very influential church leader, promulgated the error of a distinction between the two groups by placing the clergy in an elevated status above the laity. By this time an evolution in church leadership had taken place. It had undergone a metamorphosis: From *giving counsel* to *giving guidance*, then *direction* and finally to *managing* and *controlling* every aspect of church life.

Apostolic Constitutions

In the fourth century, the Apostolic Constitutions, a series of manuals purported to have been passed down from the first century by the early church fathers, viewed the **laos** as mere spectators. **Laos** took on the meaning of *laymen*—the unbiblical concept of a **laikos**. The **kleros** became men in church offices who were referred to as *clergy*. With these aberrations in place, it seemed that nothing could stop the further advance of the flawed system. The clergy began to reorganize the New Testament church until it resembled the Old Testament Levitical structure. The Law of First Intent was completely eclipsed. Successors to the Apostolic leaders eventually reinstated the very thing Jesus gave 3½ years of His life to rectify. The earthly ministry of Jesus Christ was built on the Law of First Intent. Under His Father's leadership, He had created a perfect model that He both lived and then passed on to the Twelve. It was that model that enabled the early church to conquer the world.

One might wonder: Does the altered model under which the modern day church operates actually **hinder** the further advance of the Gospel?

The New Testament Model for the Church

Let us return to the New Testament where the Apostle Paul tells us in no uncertain terms that what he had learned did not come from men, but from God.

> *But I make known to you, brethren, that the gospel which was preached by me is not according to man. For I neither received it from man, nor was I taught it, but it came through the revelation of Jesus Christ.*
> *Galatians 1:11,12*

Some have wondered why Jesus gave over 3 years of His life to the training of twelve men, and then gave us a New Testament written primarily about the ministry of Paul, who was not one of the Twelve. But the New Testament by and large deals with the expansion of the Church. Perhaps it took a hostile Pharisee, like

Paul, to see the error, since he was sent to the desert for fifteen years to be taught by Jesus Himself. He then faithfully guided the New Testament church to *prevent* violation of the Law of First Intent. Paul gave us a model for the New Testament church in his letter to the Ephesians.

And He Himself gave some to be apostles, some prophets, some evangelists, and some pastors and teachers, for the equipping of the saints for the work of ministry, for the edifying of the body of Christ.
Ephesians 4:11,12

Gifted Men Within the Model

When the Holy Spirit invades a person's life, He always bestows a spiritual gift, or gifts. These gifts enable that believer to function with a divine power or anointing, which others without that gift may lack. ***These gifted men are charged with helping other saints lacking that gift in the area of their own giftedness.*** Some of the gifts and the roles they imply are listed in Ephesians. They appear to function in the following manner:

- **Apostles**—Carry the Gospel to places it has never gone.
- **Prophets**—Unquestionably hear messages from God and stand for truth unmoved— even if it means death.
- **Evangelists**—Plainly present the Gospel to those who have never heard the message of Salvation.
- **Pastors**—Shepherd God's people with compassion and mercy, and find great joy as they minister to others' needs.
- **Teachers**—Clearly communicate truth, even complex things, simply enough that almost anyone can understand.

p^{the}RiestHOOD
^{of}eveRy BeLieveR

All these gifts are needed to penetrate the world with the message of God's love, and to raise up a priesthood of mature believers equipped to represent God to a lost world.

The five gifts listed in Ephesians 4 are *functional* in nature and not *positions* of authority. *Everyone has a gift, but no single person has all the gifts.* This assures that everyone has something to contribute to the Body, and since no single individual has all the gifts, each of us has things we can learn from other gifted people.

Every Gifted Leader Has The Same Job Description

Notice very carefully: ***These gifted leaders—apostles, prophets, evangelists, pastors and teachers—have the same job description.*** They are to ***train*** the saints or their fellow priests in the area of their giftedness. For example, even though a person is not *gifted* in evangelism, he or she still has the *responsibility* to be a fisher of men. So, the Lord gave certain people the gift of evangelism and charged them to equip and train the other saints to present the Gospel to people who have never heard the Good News of Salvation.

Those with the gift of evangelism are to share their gift with others. These others will soon be able to open the Bible and help still others to see the fact of sin, the penalty for sin and how Jesus' death paid the penalty for their sin. Disciples being trained in evangelism by evangelists are then able to experience the joy of watching a person take the final step of receiving Christ. This is God's plan to fulfill His promise to make us fishers of men. No believer can ever proffer the excuse that he or she does not have the gift of evangelism, for this is the very reason God has placed those who *do* have the gift around him or her.

Finally, it needs to be underscored that for a gifted evangelist to simply practice his gift without training others to evangelize is an *incomplete use of the gift*. Unfortunately, this is the model most often seen among the people of God today. Interdependence is an essential ingredient in the unity of the Body: *Each of us needs the gifting of others in order to be complete and to function properly.*

Every Saint Has The Same Job Description

As we have seen, every saint or priest is to be involved in doing the work of ministry and edifying the Body of Christ. This is the real reason we remain on earth for a short while after having entered into a personal relationship with God: *He has an objective for us*. He used someone to bring the message of His love to us, and now, as His disciples, God wants us to carry the message of His love to others.

No one is excluded from the task of advancing God's Kingdom. If we understand the Law of First Intent, we know that God has placed gifted people over us who are charged with our training. It was never God's intention for us to be able to hire other people to carry out His mandate on our behalf! God needs a **kingdom of priests** to reach the world. That was His plan in the beginning, and it continues to be His plan today. The Bible has correctly said that God is the same yesterday, today, and forever! He has spoken, and He never changes His mind.

A Fatal or Demonic Comma

Satan has delivered a fatal blow to the Body of Christ. A story about a shopping trip may serve to illustrate this:

A woman was out shopping and sent a text message to her husband:

"Found a $5,000 dress on sale for $500. May I buy it?" Her husband sent a text message in response: "No price is too high."

After reading his message, the woman bought the dress. The husband, however, was upset when he learned she had bought it. His wife said, "But you said no price was too high."

The husband failed to put a comma after "no" in his abbreviated text message: "No, price is too high." The comma would have clarified his answer.

In Ephesians 4:12, we see the same fatal error—the comma that changed the world. Notice again these verses in the King James Version:

And he gave some, apostles; and some, prophets; and some, evangelists; and some, pastors and teachers; For the perfecting of the saints, for the work of the ministry, for the edifying of the body of Christ.
Ephesians 4:11,12 (KJV)

In this translation a comma is placed behind the words "saints, and for the work of ministry," these commas make the gifted men responsible for three things:
- Equipping the saints
- The work of the ministry
- Edifying the Body of Christ

These commas have been used effectively by our enemy to return the church to a kingdom of clergy, where those in ecclesiastical authority do everything for the saints. Without the comma, those gifted men have just one responsibility: *To equip (or perfect) the saints.* Let's read the passage again without the commas.

> *And He Himself gave some to be apostles, some prophets, some evangelists, and some pastors and teachers, for the equipping of the saints for the work of ministry, for the edifying of the body of Christ.*
> *Ephesians 4:11,12 (NKJV)*

The saints too have but one responsibility—***the work of ministry and the edifying of the body of Christ***, as they carry out their priestly functions.

The Greek Text Has No Punctuation Marks

In the original Greek text there are no commas in this part of the passage. Translators inserted punctuation marks to help clarify the meaning of Scripture. Some translators, under the influence of the clergy/laity model, misunderstood the text and punctuated it accordingly. They did not translate according to the Law of First Intent. Some of the modern translations do not place the comma and correctly interpret it (NKJV, NIV, NASB).

A look at church history suggests that by the end of the first century, the church had become structured into a hierarchy of clergy and laity, effectively abandoning the priesthood of every believer.

In the 16th century, the Protestant Reformation occurred. A passionate Catholic priest named Martin Luther confronted the Roman Catholic leadership with the ***theology*** of the priesthood of every believer. However, he did not address the ***structure*** that supports the clergy/laity configuration where there is a pulpit that only the clergy ministers from. The modern church pays lip service to the ***priesthood of the believer,*** but fails to take action to change its structure where everything is done for the saints by the clergy. God's plan was for the apostles, the prophets, the evangelists, and the pastors and teachers to train the saints in their priestly functions. If the priesthood of every believer were faithfully taught and obeyed, Christian believers would become the priests God intends us to be. Instead, slowly but surely, the doctrine of the priesthood of every believer has once again faded into the dark recesses of history.

The Great Reformation gave ***believer/priests*** direct access to the Scriptures, but it did not deliver the ministry into the hands of God's people. Instead, it remained entrenched in the hands of professional clergy.

In our final chapter, we will give an overview of the history of the church from Luther to the present day. The modern church, or the church of the 20th and 21st Centuries, will be our topic.

5

The Priesthood
in the 21st Century

At this point, readers of this book may be asking themselves, "Why point out all these deficiencies and offer no solutions?" In this final chapter we will attempt to synthesize our thoughts and offer some suggestions for change.

First, let us re-trace the history of the doctrine of the priesthood of the believer from the sixteenth century through the present. In 1517, Martin Luther nailed his famous Ninety-Five Theses on the door of the Wittenberg Church. This resulted in what we know today as the Great Reformation. The tenets of this reform were:

• The just shall live by faith
• The priesthood of every believer

- The confession of sin directly to God
- The right and responsibility of the individual to study the Bible
- The involvement of the individual in the work of ministry
- The right of the individual to administer the sacraments

Since that day the Protestant church has given mental assent to these important doctrines, but in reality has continued to function within a clergy/laity framework. As a result, the people of God are confused—they no longer know who they are or what to believe.

One of the ways we can begin to clarify the issue is to point God's people back to their rich heritage, stemming from the reformation, and discontinue the use of the unbiblical language of clergy/laity and its accompanying concepts. Biblical vocabulary teaches a peer relationship of all true believers in Christ. Biblical words such as *saints, disciples, believers,* etc., describe **functional**, not **positional** relationships. By substituting non-Biblical language, the church creates confusion. As a result, it has perpetuated a non-Biblical structure. This was never a part of God's blueprint for the New Testament church.

During Jesus' life and ministry He focused on making disciples. In the New Testament, we are called *disciples* 269 times. Matthew teaches clearly that the imperative of the Great Commission is to *make disciples, not just converts.* **Every believer** (not just the professional clergy) is commanded to **be a disciple** and to **make disciples**. If the church were to focus on what Jesus taught, it would help solve the continuing confusion. Jesus did not build His own ministry on the clergy/laity distinction. Instead He made disciples who understood their priestly calling and ministry, disciples He carefully instructed in the winning and discipling of others. Of what value is it to teach believers that they are *laity*, when Jesus said, "I have made you **kings and priests**?" When the church recast Jesus' original plan it forged a persistent obstacle, one that will continue to impede its progress for as long as it only pays lip service to the priesthood of every believer rather than putting it into action.

Jesus is our High Priest and Lord. It is He Who bestowed on us our calling as a kingdom of priests, returning us to the Law of First Intent. This is the law that clarifies the questions, **Who** am I?, **Why** am I here?, and **What** am I to be doing? Commitment to the priesthood of the believer clarifies our calling, provides our purpose and superintends our sojourn during this earthly life. The doctrine of the priesthood delivers us from a world of relativism—seeking significance and purpose on our own. Altering God's plan has always led mankind astray.

Implications of Teaching a Clergy/Laity Model

When we govern the New Testament church in an Old Testament Levitical mode we create both theological and practical problems:

1. A clergy/laity structure resists Jesus' teaching in Revelation 1:4-6 regarding the priesthood of every believer.

    *John, to the seven churches which are in Asia: Grace to you and peace from Him who is and who was and who is to come, and from the seven Spirits who are before His throne, and from Jesus Christ, the faithful witness, the firstborn from the dead, and the ruler over the kings of the earth. To Him who loved us and washed us from our sins in His own blood, and has made us **kings and priests** to His God and Father, to Him be glory and dominion forever and ever. Amen.*
    Revelation 1:4-6

2. A clergy/laity distinction opposes the New Testament teaching of the priesthood of every believer and resuscitates something the death and resurrection of Christ rendered obsolete.

> *When He said, "A new covenant," He has made the first obsolete. But whatever is becoming obsolete and growing old is ready to disappear.*
>
> *Hebrews 8:13 (NASB)*

3. A clergy/laity distinction ignores the rent veil that grants *every* believer in Christ access to the presence of God, and not just a select few.

4. A clergy/laity distinction denies the sufficiency of the death and resurrection of Christ, which established the priesthood of every believer. While each of us is given special gifts and abilities, these bring ***responsibility*** rather than privilege. The New Covenant reality is that there is no special group in the body endowed with unique privileges that are not available to all believers.

The Need For Leadership

If there truly is no distinction within the Body of Christ—meaning all believers have equal privilege and responsibility—how do we begin to alter the thinking of God's people on this score? While acknowledging the need for leadership in the church, how do we submit ourselves to one another in the interest of unity and for the purpose of discipling the nations?

Leadership and authority in the New Testament church were initially entrusted to the Apostles. Later, as the Gospel spread and churches were established, the Apostle Paul appointed **elders** who met the criteria for spiritual maturity. These elders were to lead, feed, and protect the church as well as to set examples for godliness.

The two Greek words translated *elder* are **episkopos** and **presbuteros**. These two words are used somewhat interchangeably to indicate church leaders. The Scriptures exhort us to honor, obey and emulate their godly example. A church built upon the priesthood of every believer requires **spiritual** not **secular** leadership. Jesus reminded the people of His day that the Gentiles administered and governed by exercising authority over others. They taught by mandate, not by example. Jesus commanded His followers to obey what the Pharisees taught, but warned them that "they *say* and do not *do*."

> *Therefore whatever they tell you to observe, that observe and do, but do not do according to their works; for they say, and do not do.*
> *Matthew 23:3*

Jesus clearly forbids this form of leadership among His followers. As disciples we are called to submit to the Lordship of Christ in obedience to His commands. He alone is to govern our life and conduct. Jesus modeled a form of leadership that ran contrary to the government of His day, establishing a pattern according to which **the leader is the servant of those being trained**. Jesus taught by pacesetting or demonstrating this principle. When people are loved and served by their leaders, it becomes easier for them to reproduce this model of leadership themselves.

When the Twelve were in contention over who would be the greatest, they were debating a **positional**, not a **functional** question. The problem surfaced again when the mother of James and John asked Jesus to let her two sons sit, one on His left, and one on His right. When the other ten disciples learned of this request, they were indignant. Jesus spoke so clearly to this matter, it is a tragedy that the point of His teaching is so poorly understood and applied today.

> *But Jesus called them to Himself and said, "You know that the rulers of the Gentiles lord it over them, and those who are great exercise authority over them. Yet it shall not be so among you; but whoever desires to become great among you, let him be your servant. And whoever desires to be first among you, let him be your slave—just as the Son of Man did not come to be served, but to serve, and to give His life a ransom for many.*
> *Matthew 20:25-28*

Servant leadership is relatively easy to submit to because servant leaders are seeking to clarify God's will and plan. This leadership style prepares disciples to carry out their priestly functions, bringing freedom, blessing and joy to their lives.

What might Jesus say to church leaders and their congregations whose model conflicts with His plan—a model which does not produce the intended results?

> *But why do you call Me Lord, Lord, and do not do the things which I say? Whoever comes to Me, and hears My sayings and does them, I will show you whom he is like: He is like a man building a house, who dug deep and laid the foundation on the rock. And when the flood arose, the stream beat vehemently against that house,*

*and could not shake it, for it was founded on the rock.
But he who heard and did nothing is like a man who
built a house on the earth without a foundation, against
which the stream beat vehemently; and immediately it
fell. And the ruin of that house was great.*
Luke 6:46-49

Jesus said, "Upon this rock I will build my church." In this book
we have tried to outline some of the **foundations** upon which
Jesus built His church. One of those strong foundations is the
priesthood of every believer. A discipling priest teaches exactly
what his Master taught him. He is not free to adapt the teaching
of Jesus to suit his own tastes. Perhaps this is what initiated
Jesus' question, "Why do you call me Lord, Lord, and do not do
the things which I say?"

It is interesting to note the context in which Jesus framed that
question. Jesus said, "Whoever comes to Me, and hears My sayings
and does them, I will show you whom he is like: He is like a man
who dug deep and built his house on a foundation of rock, which
no storm could destroy." **Our obedience to Jesus' command
becomes a foundation of rock.** When we hear and do not obey,
we are like the man who built his house without a foundation.
When the storm comes, it falls. **Our disobedience to Jesus'
command becomes a foundation of sand.** One may engage in
many forms of activity, but without lasting productivity where
the fulfilling of the Great Commission is concerned. The **Great
Omission** best characterizes this disciple's life and ministry.

We have sought to show that what Jesus taught and commanded
produces a rock-solid foundation. When we choose to modify
His mandate, we are building on sand. We might ask ourselves,
"What kind of people am I producing? Is my life built on rock or on
sand?" The following chart may help answer that question.

ROCK vs.	SAND
Priest	Layman
Doers	Hearers
Great Commission	Great Omission
Eternal	Temporal
Relationship	Religion
Shema a reality	Shema a philosophy
Fisher of men	Non-fisher of men
Disciplemaker	Non-disciplemaker
Walk in the Spirit	Walk in the Flesh
N.T. Priesthood *(Ephesians 4:11,12)*	O.T. Priesthood *(Levitical Priesthood)*

We could go on with this comparison, but the meaning is surely clear. If Jesus were to evaluate our lives and ministry, would He conclude we are building on rock or sand? After evaluating His generation, Jesus gave them a clear and simple message: **Repent**. Is that His message to us today?

God Holds Us Accountable

Time and again in the Old Testament God tries and evaluates His people—all are under His authority and held accountable. The evaluation is always contingent upon God's commandments and the people's obedience or disobedience to them. The Scriptures teach that our generation will be judged in like manner.

> *For we must all appear before the judgment seat of Christ,*
> *that each one may receive the things done in the body,*
> *according to what he has done, whether good or bad.*
> *II Corinthians 5:10*

Hebrews 9:27 reminds us of our appointment with God for judgment when we shall account for the stewardship of our lives and ministry. The Apostle John was told by Jesus to remind the seven churches of Asia that He knew what they were doing. Jesus said, "I know your works." The churches at Smyrna and Philadelphia received a commendation as a result of their evaluation. Ephesus, Pergamos and Thyatira also received commendation, but also a strong rebuke in these words; "I have somewhat against you." There was obvious error that had not been dealt with in those churches. Sardis and Laodicea received no commendation, but instead a very stern rebuke because they were not operating according to the commandments of God. They were following their own designs. Jesus uses the analogy of spitting or spewing them out of His mouth. In effect, this church made Him sick to His stomach!

However, notice that this rebuke came with the assurance of God's love for them. He stood lovingly and patiently, knocking at the door, awaiting their repentance, and calling them to overcome. He was examining them in order to detect error or deviation from His original plan. The purpose of God's assessment is always to bring about **correction**. His grace always has our best interests at heart—God is for us, not against us.

As we have noted throughout this book, the problem of the priesthood of every believer as it relates to the clergy/laity model is a longstanding one. It has been debated for nearly 500 years. We have sought to establish clearly that God's plan for the New Testament church was built on the firm foundation of this truth. When a contemporary disciple operates outside God's ideal structure, is he still a disciple of Jesus, since he acts in ignorance or defiance of His will? Jesus Himself asks the penetrating question, "Why do you call me Lord, Lord, and do not the things I say?"

When God created us, He created us with emotions, a mind, and a will. As we exercise our free will, we can bring honor and glory to Him by our decisions to obey Him. Someday we will account for the decisions we have made. If we turn a deaf ear to this issue—one of many we will have to answer when we stand before our Master—the Scriptures assure us that we will be rebuked for our disobedience. A true disciple of Jesus Christ ought to have a burning passion to accurately practice and communicate the teaching of his Savior and Lord. The priesthood of every believer was a major foundation stone of the first century church, and a key to the fulfilling of the Great Commission in their generation. Guiding the New Testament church back into an Old Testament Levitical clergy/laity model will not earn us that commendation we all long to hear: "Well done, thou good and faithful servant."

During a recent pastors' conference, each pastor was asked to write a two or three sentence paragraph on the objective he understood Jesus had given to the eleven disciples to guide their ministry after He had returned to heaven. Then, based upon this objective, they were to write out their own job descriptions. The purpose of the exercise was to help these pastors recognize that Jesus had given them a clear objective in His Word, so they could evaluate their work. If they happened to be confused about what they were doing, it was hoped this exercise would help clarify to them what He had commanded them to do.

Perhaps it would be helpful for the reader to complete a similar exercise. A comparison of answers can then be made to the pages of Holy Scripture. Each of the four Gospel writers spoke clearly concerning this objective.

Then Jesus came and spoke to them, saying, "All authority has been given to Me in heaven and on earth. Go therefore and make disciples of all the nations, baptizing them in the name of the Father and of the Son and of the Holy Spirit, teaching them to observe all things that I have commanded you; and lo, I am with you always, even to the end of the age."
Matthew 28:18-20

And He said to them, "Go into all the world and preach the gospel to every creature." Mark 16:15

"...and that repentance and remission of sins should be preached in His name to all nations, beginning at Jerusalem."
Luke 24:47

Then Jesus said to them again, "Peace to you! As the Father has sent Me, I also send you."
John 20:21

"But you shall receive power when the Holy Spirit has come upon you; and you shall be witnesses to Me in Jerusalem, and in all Judea and Samaria, and to the end of the earth."
Acts 1:8

It is from these passages we derive our understanding of what has come to be known as the Great Commission. These were Jesus' final marching orders to the eleven disciples before He ascended into Heaven. It is inconceivable that He would have instructed them to do something that was impossible for them to accomplish! They were charged with the responsibility of teaching Jesus' objective for the lives of succeeding generations. A study of these five passages leads to a unified understanding of the Great Commission.

Elements of the Great Commission

- **Matthew**—Go, make disciples, baptize, teach them to obey what Christ commanded
- **Mark**—Preach the Gospel to all the world and every creature
- **Luke**—Repentance and remission of sin is to be preached starting in Jerusalem
- **John**—As the Father sent Jesus, so He sends us
- **Acts**—The Holy Spirit will empower each of us to be witnesses, beginning in Jerusalem and spreading to the ends of the earth

An Objective or Job Description

On the basis of these injunctions, a job description or statement of objectives can be formulated. Here is a sample where we take the basic commands in each of these five passages so that we can come up with a simple statement that will guide us in writing a job description:

"Jesus has sent me in the power of the Holy Spirit from my Jerusalem to all the nations of the world. He has further instructed me to preach a gospel of repentance and remission of sin, and to train my converts to become disciples who are baptized and who then obey all that Jesus has commanded. Finally, Jesus has sent me to raise up a band of disciples who will exchange their lives for the fulfilling of His Great Commission."

The people of God have not been sent to build the church. Jesus said, "*I will build my church.*" We have been commanded to make disciples whom Jesus can then use to build the church. The Eleven raised up a band of disciples who reached their world for the cause of Christ.

> *...because of the hope which is laid up for you in heaven, of which you heard before in the word of the truth of the gospel, which has come to you, as it has also in all the world, and is bringing forth fruit, as it is also among you since the day you heard and knew the grace of God in truth...*
>
> *Colossians 1:5,6*

Paul, who was trained by Jesus, stated the objective this way:

> *So naturally we proclaim Christ! We warn everyone we meet and we teach everyone we can, all that we know about Him, so that, if possible, we may bring every man*

up to his full maturity in Christ. This is what I am working at all the time, with all the strength that God gives me.

Colossians 1:28,29 (JBP)

Note the fundamentals of Paul's objectives:

- Proclaim Christ to everyone we meet—**Evangelism**
- Teach all we know about Christ—**Discipleship**
- Bring everyone to his full maturity in Christ—
  Disciplemaking

To underscore: *A mature disciple understands his priestly calling and responsibilities.* The Great Commandment balanced with the Great Commission characterizes his life. A mature disciple is not living the Great Omission; he is leading a band of disciples in the fulfillment of the Great Commission. This is the objective that ought to guide every believer and every assembly of believers. John added further clarification to this concept of maturity in his First Epistle:

> *I write to you, **fathers**, because you have known Him who is from the beginning. I write to you, **young men**, because you have overcome the wicked one. I write to you, **little children**, because you have known the Father.*
> *I John 2:13*

In this passage John suggests three stages of maturity.

- **Fathers**
- **Young men**
- **Children**

Later the Apostle Paul added a fourth stage of maturity for us:

- **Elders**

    *So when they had appointed elders in every church, and
    prayed with fasting, they commended them to the Lord
    in whom they had believed.*
    Acts 14:23

Elders, as we previously noted, were disciples who were
ordained—set apart—to serve and give guidance to the newly
formed churches. They were to ensure that growth and maturity
took place in the lives of disciples so they could win and disciple
their cities for Christ.

Applying These Principles: A Personal Example

During my years of ministry in Singapore, I used these four stages
to guide me in bringing people to their full maturity. It helped me
evaluate the maturation of every person that God entrusted me
to disciple. The chart below contains the terminology I derived
from Scripture and used in the process of evaluation.

Children	Convert
Young Men	Disciple
Fathers	Disciplemaker
Elders	Leaders of Disciplemakers

Convert

When we led people to Christ we considered them converts or spiritual children. Since Jesus said we were to make disciples, not converts, we felt an obligation to establish these converts in their relationship with God. Guided by the ***Shema***, our converts were taught to read, study and memorize the Word of God. We were not content with converts simply attending church services (although that was encouraged). As spiritual parents we took seriously our responsibility to feed, protect and to teach our converts to walk with God on a daily basis. We helped them find Bible-teaching congregations, where they could worship corporately and fellowship with other believers.

To guide this discipling process, we developed a set of profiles. These served to orient us as we helped our converts to become mature, reproducing disciples. Sample copies of these four profiles are found in the appendix of this book.

Disciple

When a convert became a disciple, we turned to a second profile to help guide their growth. We began to train them in the Great Commission. We taught them how to open the Bible and share the Gospel message of repentance and how to help others receive Jesus into their lives. We also taught them how to follow-up their converts. Here, the focus was on training in evangelism and the early stages of discipleship.

Disciplemakers

Once a disciple had helped two other persons mature as disciples, we designated him/her a disciplemaker. Using a third profile, we continued helping them to mature, and gave them a limited leadership role under another mature leader. This leader began to train them in leadership skills, character development and advanced follow-up. The goal was to help the new disciplemaker become more effective in multiplying spiritually.

Leaders of Disciplemakers

When someone had completed the disciplemaker profile he became a leader and maker of disciplemakers. At this point he had reached the *elder* stage and was trained for a lifetime involvement in the accomplishing of Great Commission objectives. In our ministry, these people were considered mature enough for us to delegate Great Commission responsibilities to their leadership. We focused on helping them master the message of the Bible so they were providing accurate Biblical directions to the teams they were serving. Every person involved in this ministry in Singapore had someone assigned to him/her to ensure that he/she came to full maturity in Christ.

Each year the various team leaders, using their profiles, were asked to prayerfully make these projections:

- How many people their team was trusting God to win that year
- How many of the converts on their team would mature and become disciples
- How many of the disciples on their team would become disciplemakers
- How many of the disciplemakers on their team would mature enough to become leaders of disciplemakers

Like Paul, the objective was to bring everyone to his/her full maturity in Christ. The projections and profiles that were used were never meant to put people in boxes, but rather to guide disciples and ensure that their team members were growing in Christ. It helped us gauge whether we were accomplishing the objective set for us—the training of priests. This was the mission that Jesus had given us to complete.

Maturity vs. Numbers

Many leaders of ministries today measure success in terms of quantity or numbers, rather than maturity. Just because a person has been in church or involved in a particular ministry for five years does not necessarily mean that person has five years of maturity. Gauging or measuring maturity, as difficult as it may seem, results in a growing and multiplying ministry. The Apostle Paul, writing to his young son in the faith, Timothy, describes four generations of disciples in his ministry:

> *And the things that you have heard from me among many witnesses, commit these to faithful men who will be able to teach others also.*
> *II Timothy 2:2*

In this letter, Paul helps us understand the progression of disciplemaking by allowing us to observe his own strategy. Using the maturity levels we have already examined, we can see that Paul practiced what he preached.

> *So when they had appointed elders in every church, and prayed with fasting, they commended them to the Lord in whom they had believed.*
> *Acts 14:23*

Paul	Elders	Leaders of Disciplemakers
Timothy	Fathers	Disciplemaker
Faithful Men	Young Men	Disciple
Others Also	Children	Convert

In Singapore, we saw a small team of fifteen young men and women disciples, who had committed themselves to serve Christ, grow into a small army of over 1,000 men and women functioning as priests in just over twelve years. Because of our ministry, and because so many joined churches in Singapore, I was asked to codify some of these principles. This resulted in the production of a training course titled, **Equipping The Saints**, which is now used in over 60 countries of the world.

Many church and ministry leaders seem to count:

- How many were in Sunday school or other congregational units
- How many attended meetings
- How many came forward at an invitation
- How many were baptized or confirmed
- How many joined the church
- How many foreign missionaries are supported
- How many types of ministries are operating within the church
- How many have pledged to the building project
- How much is given in the weekly offerings

Obviously this is not an exhaustive list, but it reflects our preoccupation with matters not emphasized by Jesus. The Scriptures never emphasize *quantity*; they do, however, insist on *quality* of life! Numbers are insignificant; spiritual maturity and spiritual reproduction are on the heart of God. His value system is to become our value system. But how do we deepen our understanding of this concept?

Reproduction is the Sign of Maturity

• Physical Reproduction

God's first commandment to Adam in Genesis 1:28 was, "...be fruitful and multiply and replenish the earth." In Genesis 1:11, we read that God made every living thing with a seed within itself, so that under the right conditions it was able to reproduce.

> *Then God said, "Let the earth bring forth grass, the herb that yields seed, and the fruit tree that yields fruit according to its kind, whose seed is in itself, on the earth"; and it was so.*
>
> *Genesis 1:11*

Not only were the things of the earth to reproduce, but God intended His ultimate creation, Man, to reproduce. In Genesis 2, God created Eve from Adam's side. God did not want Adam to be alone. Their union made physical reproduction possible, so Adam and Eve could live in accordance with God's commandment. But God also had in mind another type of reproduction, described later in Scripture.

• **Spiritual Reproduction**

In John 15, we learn that God also created us to be spiritually reproductive. As we abide in union with Christ through our devotional life and through our obedience to Him, we become fruitful and spiritually reproductive. Jesus makes us fruitful as fishers of men, and reproductive through disciplemaking. We are delivered from being spiritually sterile. Activity becomes productivity. Abiding in Christ reinforces our understanding of *Who* we are, *Why* we are here, and *What* we are to be doing—performing priestly tasks.

Activity vs. Productivity

There are many kinds of worthwhile ministry opportunities that exist in the church today. Singing in the choir, directing choir, teaching Sunday school, leading Bible study groups or working among youth are all excellent examples. But nowhere in Scripture are these activities prescribed for us. What we *are* instructed to do is make disciples (Matthew 28). The reason we participate in any activity is to bring us into contact with those who are seeking answers to life's questions.

Churches today are filled with lost people and others in search of someone to disciple them. *Many in church may know about God* and yet have no idea how to *know Christ personally*. There are those who begin going to church and who become involved in various activities hoping to find God. It has been said that we live in a fatherless generation, and that is probably true both physically and spiritually. Spiritual fathers and mothers, if they are willing to be used by God, have opportunity to disciple the scores of young men and women waiting for someone to take interest in them.

priesthood
of every believer

Many converts, after they have trusted Christ, are simply told to keep coming back to church. When they do so, they may only observe people who show up weekly, pay tithes and offerings and leave ministry to the professionals. What a new believer needs is a caring mentor to take a personal interest in him and to begin to disciple him. As this begins to happen, converts become disciples, disciples become disciplemakers, and the cycle continues through multiple generations. It is quite possible within existing structures to see a true believer/priesthood emerge and begin to function as Christ intends.

Mistaking activity for authentic ministry is a satanic ploy. It robs God's people of getting in on what God is doing. It results in a loss of productivity, due to a false sense of accomplishment. God's plan for us has always been to be spiritually reproductive, not simply involved in religious activities. Each believer needs to take inventory from time to time to discern whether he or she is engaging in activity for activity's sake, or because those activities are fishing ponds for Jesus—places to connect with those in need.

Outside the existing structures, there is a plethora of opportunities awaiting Christ's disciple/priests. Here, in the church without walls, we do not wait for someone to come to us. We obey the injunction, "go and make disciples". In the Greek language, the verb 'go' means *as you are going*. As we live real life in real places, we walk in the Spirit and listen and watch for opportunities to serve people, meet needs, and eventually see the Lord open doors for evangelism.

God has placed us as His priests in our homes, neighborhoods, schools, shops, manufacturing facilities, hospitals, and even prisons to function productively for Him. We are to be the aroma of Christ in all these places. We are each called to **full-time ministry**—cleverly cloaked in the garb of a teacher, lawyer, clerk or some other worker. These settings become our pulpits, from which we ever hold forth the Good News of the Gospel.

This book calls for a radical rethinking of the foundation upon which we are building the church of Jesus Christ—and particularly its infrastructure. History affirms that we have built upon sand and not rock. A few early church leaders took it upon themselves to teach what was expedient for them. They disregarded what Jesus both taught and practiced during His life and ministry as He trained the Twelve. Sadly we are feeling the effects of those decisions to this very day.

It is distressing that many scholarly theologians have turned a blind eye to the doctrine of the priesthood of every believer. Refusing to confront a distorted clergy/laity structure functioning in so many of our churches, they exacerbate the church's inability to fulfill the Great Commission. A clergy/laity doctrine has allowed professional clergy to distort to their own advantage what Jesus taught and practiced. Jesus taught and made every disciple a priest. The church has taught that only professional clergy can perform priestly functions. Historically, laymen have not been allowed to carry out priestly functions because they have been deemed uneducated and not qualified to perform sacred duties. Their leaders have abandoned their delegated responsibility to equip them to do the work of ministry.

Restructuring the model of ministry has turned a powerful army of priests—who in history past turned the world upside down—into a *visionless* laity who have lost their identity and now no longer comprehend **Who** they are, **Why** they are here or **What** they are to do.

p^{the}RiestHood
^{of}eveRY BeLieveR

Throughout history, Biblical disciples have thanked God for allowing the Holy Spirit of God to burn this vision into the heart of a small remnant who have kept it alive and who have continued to train saints to do the work of ministry as instructed by the King. *It is time once again for believer/priests—those who understand and embrace this concept—to rise up and challenge the clergy/laity paradigm.*

God is waiting for a resurgence of obedience to this supreme command. While we pray for revival—and surely it will come— we can hasten that day by preparing an army for the outpouring of God's Spirit upon a lost and dying world. When the harvest of the age begins, who will be ready to follow up and disciple those who will respond to the eternal message of hope?

Dear Reader, as you evaluate your life and ministry, be sure that they reflect the mission given by Jesus in the four Gospels and the book of Acts. If you are part of God's remnant, your life and ministry ought to be characterized by raising up disciples who:

- Understand they are *priests*, and not *laymen*.
- Are being *trained* to win others and disciple them.
- Are actively *engaged* in a ministry of discipleship.
- Are *fruitful*, reproducing disciples.
- Have a life and ministry *balanced* by the Great Commandment to love God and the Great Commission to love others by winning and discipling.

May God grant us all grace, mercy and strength to apply ourselves to engage in the battle for the minds and souls of men and women. May He give us a band of disciples in exchange for our lives even as He did our Lord Jesus Christ.

For the past twenty-five years I have given myself to training pastors and mission organizations who are looking for help in how to re-structure their ministries according to the New Testament model. I would never write on such a controversial issue without being willing to offer aid. I have produced a training course entitled *Equipping The Saints*, a codification of what I did in the ministry in Singapore. It is available in over 32 languages, and is being used in over 60 countries around the world. If you have need of such help, and do not know where to turn, you can reach me at this email address: ETSUSA@aol.com, or call my office at 903-455-3782. The ministry offices of *Equipping The Saints* are located at 4006 Walnut Street, Greenville, TX 75401.

—Appendix—
ETS Ministry Profile Guides

ETS Convert Profile

Date Started: _____

1. Has completed all four lessons in Studies in John. ❐

2. Has memorized five assurance verses; New Convert Profile Lessons 1/1-1/5. ❐

3. Has completed Bible Studies on assurance, New Convert Profile 1/1-1/15. ❐

4. Identifies with other Christians.
   Goes to church_____
   Has been baptized _____
   Declares, "I am a Christian" _____ ❐

Date Completed: _____

ETS Disciple Profile

Date Started: _____

1. Puts Christ first in the major areas of life, taking steps to separate from sin: ❐

Reputation	**Location**	**Money/Possessions**
Friends	**Leisure**	**Self (Personality, Mind, Body**
Career	**Education**	**Relationships (Opposite Sex)**

2. Has a consistent daily devotional time and is developing a prayer life. ❐

3. Demonstrates faithfulness and desire to learn and applies the Word of God through regular Bible Study and Scripture Memory. ❐

4. Has completed ETS Book 1 & 2. ❐

5. Manifests a heart for witnessing, gives a testimony and presents the Bridge regularly with increasing skill. ❐

6. Demonstrates a servant heart and a sincere interest in helping others. ❐

7. Attends church and maintains close ties (where practical) with a local ETS fellowship displaying love and unity. ❐

8. Is a learner—open and teachable. ❐

Date Completed: _____

ETS Disciplemaker Profile

Date Started: _____

1. Evidences growth in the virtues and skills under our Profile of an ETS Disciple. ❐

2. Demonstrates an ability to lead people to Christ personally. ❐

3. Is the prime influence in raising up two or more

Christians who meet the qualifications of our Profile of a ETS Disciple. ☐

Names of Christians who have become ETS Disciples:

a)

b)

4. Is currently engaged in the task of disciplemaking. ☐

5. Completed ETS Book 3 and is continuing in Bible Study. ☐

Date Completed: _____

ETS Leader of Disciplemakers Profile

Date Started: _____

1. Evidences growth in the virtues and skills under our Profile of a ETS Disciplemaker. ☐

2. Demonstrates commitment, capacity and gifts to initiate a ministry with both individuals and groups and is doing so. ☐

3. Believes God wants him or her to be a faithful, available, teachable person who gives leadership in the ministry of disciplemaking and is doing so. ☐

4. Is a team leader who can recruit, band, develop and lead people in accomplishing the Great Commission ☐

objectives and is doing so. ❏

5. Has completed ETS Book 4. ❏

6. Reproduced at least three generations deep. ❏

Date Completed: _____

ETS Convert Follow-Up Guide Profile

1. I (the trainer) am currently praying for this convert. ❑

2. My convert has assurance of salvation. ❑
   - We have gone through the Bridge Illustration
     together and he/she understands the Gospel
     as presented in 1/7. ❑
   - Has memorized 1 John 5:11-13. ❑
   - Has completed Assurance of Salvation Bible Study 1/4. ❑
   - I have gone through the lesson on Assurance in 1/9 ❑
     to make sure my convert understands assurance of
     salvation. ❑
   - Has expressed a real Assurance of Salvation. ❑

Date Completed: _____

3. My convert is having a Quiet Time. ❑
   - We have discussed the importance of a Quiet Time
     1/10 and completed the Appointment with God
     assignment. ❑
   - Has completed all Appointment With God
     assignments 1/10-1/14 ❑
   - We have had, or shared, our Quiet Time together at
     least twice. ❑

Date Completed: _____

4. My convert realizes the need for Christian fellowship. ❑
   - We have discussed the principle of fellowship from
     Hebrews 10:24,25 and Matthew 18:20. ❑

- Meets and identifies with Christians. ☐
- Has a church home or is praying about one. ☐

5. My convert has memorized all 5 of the Assurance Verses. ☐
  - Outside Reading Assignments 1/4-1/8 Beginning With Christ. ☐
  - Has read the complete series, Beginning With Christ, 1/4-1/8, and we have discussed each verse and its meaning. ☐
  - Has correctly quoted to me all five verses with the references in one setting. ☐

6. My convert has finished Lessons on Assurance Bible Study 1/4-1/8. ☐
  - We have discussed the five lessons. ☐

7. My convert has evidenced new life in Christ and demonstrates a desire to mature in Christ. This is evidenced by his/her: ☐
  - Owning and reading a New Testament. ☐
  - Having a Quiet Time regularly. ☐
  - Sharing his/her conversion with others. ☐

8. My convert's desire to grow has been demonstrated by:
  - Completion of Book 1 in ETS. ☐

9. We have spent time together in at least two secular activities.
  Name of activity:
  (1) ☐

  (2) ☐

10. My immediate leader knows this person and has gone through this guide with me. My leader agrees that this person meets the requirements of an ETS convert. ☐

Date Completed: _____

Comments:

_____
_____
_____
_____
_____
_____
_____
_____
_____
_____
_____
_____
_____
_____
_____
_____
_____
_____
_____
_____
_____
_____
_____

ETS Disciple Follow-Up Guide Profile

1. **I (the trainer) am currently praying daily for this individual.** ☐

2. **Has made a major Lordship of Christ decision, either in a group meeting or after discussing appropriate Scriptures (Matthew 6:33, Luke 9:23) with me personally.** ☐

3. **Attempts to put Christ first in the following areas of life:** ☐

   - **Reputation**
     —Has told his/her family he/she is a Christian. ☐
     —Prays before meals in public places. ☐

   - **Money and possessions**
     —I have shared the Scriptural teaching of stewardship and he/she is giving at least 10%. ☐

   - **Self (personality, mind, body)**
     —Makes a real effort to overcome sin and weaknesses and is making progress. ☐

   - **Friends**
     —Has told non-Christian friends he/she is a Christian and is willing to separate from those who lead him/her back into sin. ☐

   - **Education**
     —Seeks God's Will through counsel. ☐
     —Doesn't let studies have priority over his daily walk with God. ☐

- **Dating**
  —Practices the Biblical standard of moral
  conduct with the opposite sex. ❏

- **Marriage**
  —Is working to have a Scriptural home. ❏

- **Career**
  —Does not let avocation hinder spiritual
  development or personal responsibility to
  fulfilling the Great Commission. ❏
  —Knows how to set objectives and is able to plan
  and schedule priorities to meet objectives. ❏

- **Leisure Time**
  —Knows the value of planning leisure time and does
  it with the Lord rather than without Him. ❏

4. **Has a consistent daily devotion time**
   —We have discussed together the Bible concept of
   Quiet Time from Lesson 1/10. ❏
   —I (the trainer) have had a minimum of two Quiet
   Times with this person. ❏
   —Has not missed more than five times in
   thirty days. ❏

5. **Is developing a prayer life**
   —We have discussed the principle of prayer from
   Lesson 1/11. ❏
   —We have discussed the use of a prayer list and has
   one in use from Lesson 1/11. ❏
   —Is presently experiencing answers
   to prayer. ❏

6. **Demonstrates faithfulness and a desire to learn and apply the Word of God through regular Bible Study and Scripture Memory**
    - —Has completed lessons on Christian living (Bible Studies 1/9-1/16). ❐
    - —Has completed Bible Studies 2/1-3/13. ❐
    - —Has completed memorizing the verses from Lessons 1/9-1/13. ❐

7. **Manifests a heart for witnessing, gives his/her testimony and shares the Gospel regularly and with increasing skill**
    - —I have shared the Biblical concept of witnessing from Lesson 1/7. ❐
    - —Has completed How to Share Your Testimony Effectively (Lesson 2/4) and has shared his/her testimony in my presence. ❐
    - —Can present the Bridge illustration with skill. ❐
    - —Has presented the Gospel and testimony once in my presence to a non-Christian, and we have afterwards evaluated the presentation. ❐
    - —Has witnessed on his/her own initiative at least three times in the last six months. ❐

8. **Demonstrates a servant's heart of sincere interest in helping others**
    - —Understands the Spiritual injunction of serving and is trying to build this area into his/her life. ❐
    - —Willingly serves as there is need. ❐

9. **Attends church regularly, displaying love and unity**

—Attends church three-fourths of the time
during the use of this checklist. ❒

10. I have gone through the ETS material on:
- Basic Christian Living (Lesson 1/9-1/15) ❒
- Personal and Spiritual Management (Lesson 1/4, 1/ 5, 2/1, 2/2, 2/5, 2/15, and 2/16) ❒
- Evangelism (Lesson 1/6, 1/7, 1/8, 2/3, 2/4, 2/6, and 2/7) ❒

11. Is a learner—open and teachable
—Is not argumentative and defensive when
corrected by me. ❒
—Is able to see the other man's point of view,
accepting and appreciating valid contributions. ❒
—Is willing to share his/her life with me, not
living behind a false veneer. ❒

12. I (the trainer) am presently meeting with this potential disciple once a month for one-to-one time (not missing more than one month in four) ❒

13. My immediate supervisor knows this individual, has gone through this checklist with me, and agrees this individual meets the requirements of an ETS disciple ❒

Date Completed: _____

Other Publications by David L. Dawson

Equipping the Saints

In use in over fifty countries of the world, ETS is a worldwide discipleship training program designed for one-on-one disciplemaking or small groups. Covering all the major principles of discipleship, ETS trains participants in their own personal walk with God and equips them to win and disciple others. Available in Adult and Youth Editions. This is a nine volume series with eight weeks of training per book.

A Visual Survey of the Bible

The Bible made simple and illustrated. The Survey presents the central message of the Bible, arranging every major event in chronological order, with the aid of a beautiful 15-foot pictorial timeline. Available in Adult, Youth, and Color Book Editions.

The Life of Christ harmonizes the 184 different events recorded by the Gospel writers into chronological order to help us better understand who Christ was and what He came to do. Recorded here are when these events occurred on the calendar, and where they happened on the map, without outside interpretation or theological bias. Together with the accompanying visual outline, this narrative brings the fractured images of Jesus together to form an intimate and powerful historical portrait.

All Books are Available from:

Equipping The Saints Ministry
4006 Walnut Street, Greenville, TX 75401
Tel (903) 455-3782 • Fax (903) 454-8524 • etsusa@aol.com
or
Great Commission Publishing
www.greatcommissionpublishing.com
or
www.christianoutfitters.com

To Contact the Author:
David L. Dawson
Equipping The Saints Ministry
(903-455-3782)
etsusa@aol.com